Also by Jay McGraw

Life Strategies for Teens
Life Strategies for Teens Workbook

Closing the Gap

A Strategy for Bringing Parents and Teens Together

Jay McGraw

FIRESIDE

New York   London   Toronto   Sydney   Singapore

FIRESIDE
Rockefeller Center
1230 Avenue of the Americas
New York, NY 10020

For information about special discounts for bulk purchases,
please contact Simon & Schuster Special Sales,
1-800-456-6798 or business@simonandschuster.com

Designed by Joy O'Meara
Interior illustrations by Benjamin Vincent

Manufactured in the United States of America

10   9   8   7   6   5   4   3   2   1

Library of Congress Cataloging-in-Publication Data is available.

ISBN 0-7432-2469-8

Contact Jay at www.jaymcgraw.com

I dedicate this book with love and gratitude to three of my biggest fans, best friends, and strongest influences. Three people who are always there and never say no. My dad, my mom, and my brother Jordan.

And to
My grandma Jerry, who doesn't hear often enough how much I love her. Grandma is just plain awesome!

And to
My uncle Scott Madsen, an enormous influence on me, and more important, the absolute embodiment of a true friend.

And to
Jan Miller, whose passion, excitement, energy, and love I depend on daily.

ACKNOWLEDGMENTS

I would like to sincerely thank my Dad for everything that he does. Thanks, Dad, for never being too busy, too tired, or too distracted. You are always excited to help and we have fun doing it. Thanks for everything, Dad, I love you.

I would also like to thank my mom. Primarily for keeping ole Dad in check. For being in my corner no matter what I am doing, and most important for all that you do to keep this place running smoothly. Thanks, Mom, I love you.

Thanks to my brother Jordan, who keeps me laughing constantly. You make me enormously proud, buddy, I love you.

I thank Wes Smith, not only for the amazing work that he contributed to this book, but also for the amazing attitude that he had in working on it. Wes, you are truly an artist. I was impressed in the beginning and amazed in the end. Wow, you truly made this book what it is.

Thank you also to Frank Lawlis for his contribution to this project and for his friendship. Frank, you too made such an enormous contribution to this book that it absolutely would not have been the same without you. I think that you probably have forgotten more than most people will ever know. Thanks for everything, Frank.

Thanks also to Dave Kahn, a real friend. Dave, you make everything easier, sure, but most important, you make this whole deal much more fun. Thanks, Dave, I love ya, man.

I proudly thank my cousin Scooter, probably my best friend of all. Scooter always has time to listen to the long version even though I constantly promise the short version. Mr. "No, no I wasn't sleeping.

What do you need?" I am truly lucky to have you for a friend. Golf this weekend?

Thank you to Bill Dawson, who is not only always willing to contribute, but more important, always does contribute. Bill is always there and I am always impressed in so many ways. Bill, you are amazing, I'm just glad you're on my side. Thanks for everything.

Thanks to Dominick Anfuso, my editor at Simon & Schuster. Dominick, as always you make these projects better and more fun. Thanks for everything, Dominick; you are a true friend.

I would like to thank Jan and Katie Davidson, true friends and supporters of everything that I do. You two are more supportive than most moms and sisters are of their own families. Thanks, guys.

Thank you does not even express the gratitude I have for Shannon Miser-Marvin. Shannon, I hope that you realize how grateful I am for all that you do. You're usually not there to hear it, but I am constantly saying, "It *will* be done. Shannon said she would take care of it." Thanks, Shannon, for everything.

Thanks to Kym Elizando. I really appreciate all that you do, Kym, thanks. Thanks also to Carla Speed.

Thank you to Paul Earnest for always supporting me in whatever I am doing. Thanks, P.E., you're the best.

Thanks to Benjamin Vincent; I am always impressed with the work you do and the amazing attitude you do it with. Thanks for everything, Ben.

Thanks also to Carolyn Reidy and Mark Gompertz at Simon & Schuster for all of the ways in which you have contributed to this project.

Thank you to Kristen McGuiness and Jennifer Love for your hard work and dedication to making this book the best it can be.

CONTENTS

Contents

10

FOREWORD

As a lifelong professional in the field of human behavior, as a parent of a 15-year-old teenager, and as a concerned adult who must live in today's world, I can tell you without reservation that *Closing the Gap: A Strategy for Bringing Parents and Teens Together,* is a critically important and timely "how to" manual. Both parents and teens can use this book to get more of what they want and need and solve a huge problem that threatens today's young people. *Closing the Gap* is an important beginning in taking teenagers of today out of harm's way.

If you are a parent, grandparent, or teenager, you *are* infected with a very serious disease. It is not a disease of biological origin, it does not attack the tissues of your body, but it is a disease, nonetheless. It is an acute social disease that attacks the fiber of your family, in particular, and our society in general.

Parents, your sons and daughters are in danger! The danger is real; it is *right now* and it spans the physical, mental, emotional, and spiritual realms.

Teens, whether you think so or not, you are in trouble here, and your parents are confused or, even worse, totally lost about how to help. They are in this dilemma because in many ways your life and world are foreign to them. Things have changed big-time since they were your age!

You both have a huge need *and* responsibility to close the gap in your relationship and find a way to make it through this time in our history.

This social disease attacks families at every level of sophistication, education, and income. It attacks families from every part of the country whether rural or urban. It is racially indiscriminate and *does not* just happen to other people you see on the local or national news. It is more likely than not that it has infected you and your family already.

The disease is one of disconnection, distraction, and fragmentation. Parents and teens, ask yourselves a few hard questions:

- When was the last time the two of you had a meaningful and open conversation about something that mattered?
- Each of you has things you are afraid of in your own lives and things you fear about and for each other. Have you talked about those concerns?
- Do you spend more time on the Internet, watching television, listening to music, or talking to friends or coworkers than to each other?
- Do you know what is going on in each other's world?
- Parents, do you know who your teen's friends are? What they are having to deal with at school? What is going on behind that closed bedroom door?
- Teens, do you know what is going on in your mother or father's world— workwise, healthwise, or financially?
- If there are younger children in the home, do either of you actively work to influence their world and where they are headed?

If your answers are not a strong "Yes," then *Closing the Gap: A Strategy for Bringing Parents and Teens Together* is a book you must read and then implement into your family and daily life.

I don't want to be some histrionic alarmist here, but in my view, we as a country are falling apart at the family level. The disease, injury, and death rate among teens is skyrocketing, with drugs and alcohol being involved in an alarmingly high percentage of the cases. Teen suicides, acts of violence, and traffic deaths are marring the lives of you and your friends and neighbors. We cannot fix all of this by passing laws, nor can we expect our schools or teachers to fix problems that have their roots in the parent–teen relationship.

But things can be fixed! They can be fixed by your taking responsibility for yourselves and for your relationship at home. You need each other and you each have important things you can give the other to ensure that each of you is successful. By learning what Jay has researched and written in these pages, you get a unique and rare perspective on the problems of today. I say "unique and rare" because this is one, if not the only, book I have ever seen that is written by a young person instead of some stuffed-shirt expert. Parents will get the insight of a young person who has navigated the current-day terrain, and teens will relate because of the realness and relevance of a message delivered by one who "gets it."

Yes, Jay is my kid and I am proud of him and what he has done here. Hey, what can I tell you—he got his brains from his mother.

—Phillip C. McGraw, Ph.D.

Closing
the Gap

WHY DIDN'T YOU MAKE ME DO RIGHT?

When Jennine first stood up, I wasn't sure if she was going to get sick or scream. She was pale and trembling. But her eyes flashed anger. The fractured bones of her life had just been laid bare by her parents. She'd made a wreck of things, so they'd brought her to my father's Life Strategies seminar looking for answers.

She'd had a baby at 17. Quit high school. Been married and divorced twice. Been in and out of drug rehab. One damn mess after another. Most recently, she'd gotten drunk, totaled her car, and crushed her leg. They'd had to replace her entire knee. The fresh bandages and lifelong scars were a constant reminder of all that she'd done wrong.

Her parents recited this sad litany as if *they'd* been the victims of a plane crash. In their minds, it was their ordeal. Not their Jennine's. The parents claimed that they'd given her "every possible advantage" as a child and as a teenager. They had done everything right, they had loved and trusted her, but now she was a 25-year-old crash-and-burn artist. They were at a loss about what to do. She couldn't get her act together, they said. They felt they were out of options. They feared that she would be dead by the year's end if allowed to continue her self-destructive course.

That's when Jeninne stood up. Her hands and arms were shaking. She looked weary and defeated at first. Shaking with emotion, she glared at her parents. For a minute, I thought Dad's seminar was going to go Jerry Springer. But this wasn't a sideshow. This was a woman who had been self-destructing but was now fighting for her life. She and her parents had allowed a huge gap to grow between them. As I watched from the back of the room, I wondered if this was their last chance to reconnect. I sensed that Jennine's time was running out.

Half sobbing, half raging, she confronted her mother and father. From deep in her gut, the rage came: "Damn you, why didn't you make me do right? Why did you let me con you? Why didn't you stand up to me like real parents? Why did you let me throw my life away when you knew better and I was being a complete moron? You had to know. You had to know, and now look at me, and look at you!"

Jennine's father and mother put their heads in their hands. The daughter came apart and crumpled into her chair. The rest of the audience went silent—even my dad, which doesn't happen very often. I could see other parents in the audience mentally retracing their own experiences with their kids. I saw a number of the younger teen girls with tears in their eyes. I'm not married. I don't have kids. I'm barely out of the "kid" years myself. But Jennine's heartbreak gave me a jolt of reality too. It brought home the point that Dad has made time and time again in his books and seminars: the things you do for your kids— and the things you *don't* do for them—have a lasting impact on their lives as adults.

Why didn't you make me do right? How does anyone know how to steer young people in the right direction? How can you give us what we need without giving us too much? How can you guide us without pushing us? Love us without smothering us?

How do you know that we need you even when we are pushing you away? How can you tell we're in trouble when we say we're fine? How can you help us learn to make the right choices when you aren't there to guide us?

No wonder parents are always saying things like "I sure wish kids came with a how-to manual." I'm just two years out of my teenager days, and I can tell you this: most teens wish they had a manual too:

How to Raise Good Parents. Parents are just as much a puzzle to teens as teens are to parents.

I know, there's been a "generation gap" since before my dad was a teenager, but it's different now. The generation gap has become a Grand Canyon with teens and parents waving at each other from opposite sides of the great divide. It's no longer about differences in hairstyles, clothing, or musical tastes. A lot of teens *wish* they had those arguments with their folks. These days, most parents don't know their teens well enough to have any idea *what* their tastes are. They don't know their teens because they don't spend time together. Parents, you can take your "quality time" and dump it at the nearest recycling center. It's not working. Do you hear me? It's not working!!

Here's a flash. I know what goes on behind the door your little darling slammed in your face last night. And let me tell you, if you don't want to know, you should know where teens go when they've got the car keys and no curfew. I know how teens strike back at their AWOL parents. I know how they lie to their parents and then laugh at them when they buy into their line of BS. I know where they go on the Internet to defy their parents' orders. I know what they do to compensate for empty home lives. I know what your parents ought to know too. And I know what you teens are doing to screw up your lives. It's not really cool and clever. It's self-destructive.

When there is no family connection, teens look outside for a group identity, support, esteem, validation, and friendships. That makes them easy marks for gangs, cults, drug dealers, and sexual predators. Just look at the headlines: Gangs have spread into suburbia. School shootings are regular occurrences. Across America, kids are hooked on heroin, crack, prescription painkillers, and Ecstasy. Crime is down nationwide, but the overall juvenile arrest rate was 7 percent higher in 1999 than in 1980. Suicide is the third leading cause of death for people between the ages of 15 and 25.

Pay attention: drugs are going to kill thousands of teens this year! And don't think that you are magically protected, you aren't! I don't know about you, but these statistics scare the hell out of me! I hope they scare you too. They're a wake-up call. But you need to understand something: just because alarms aren't going off, that doesn't mean you've got a squeaky clean, happy teen at home. Not every kid shoots up a school to signal his distress—at least not right away. Some kids retreat quietly. If your teen has withdrawn from talking to you or from interacting with other teens, you can probably assume that it's not because he or she is aspiring to a life as a cloistered monk or nun. We don't even claim to be that disciplined.

Does your teen withdraw to his or her room at every opportunity? Does she talk with you about her friends? Does he participate in discussions at meals? Does your teen want you to see projects from school? When is the last time you actually went into your teen's room and looked at what's hanging on the walls and sitting on the shelves? Have you listened to your teens' CDs to determine whether they are listening to the "edited for radio" lyrics or the uncensored nonradio versions?

Teens: Do your parents hide behind the newspaper? Do they get up and leave the room when you walk in? Do they always have to work when you have a game, a recital, or an open house at school? Do you do anything together anymore? When was the last time they took a walk, a bike ride, or even a trip to the ice-cream stand with you?

Is watching television or a movie your idea of "quality" time? Well, I'm sorry, but there's usually very little quality in that. If you aren't interacting, if you're both just staring at a screen, it's just "quantity" time. It doesn't matter if you aren't talking about topics of great importance. Talk about a game, a celebrity, a song, the weather, but keep the conversational lines open because the small talk opens channels for the important stuff that always comes out eventually.

You can't afford to coast here. Kids across the country are in serious trouble. Today's teens are in crisis. Parents, you need to know that your teenagers are in danger. Teens, you too need to sound the alarms and wake up to what's going on. The nuclear family has blown apart into a million fragments. It's flying in all directions. There are more dual-income families in America today than ever before. It used to be that only about 30 percent of homes had two wage earners. Now the figure is more like 70 percent. As a result, moms are no longer home to listen or to monitor their children's activities during the volatile teen years. Epidemic divorce rates mean that more single mothers and disappearing dads have compounded the problem.

An estimated 7 million kids are unsupervised every day between 3:30 and 5:00 P.M. during the school year. No wonder 85 percent of teen crimes take place during that same time period. A friend in the Midwest told me that when his stay-at-home wife meets her kids as they get off the school bus, the other kids in the neighborhood swarm around her because there's nobody home at their houses. Those kids are dying to tell a parent how their day went. They're dying for parental attention. And some are just dying, period. Each year in the U.S., thousands of teenagers commit suicide. Suicide is the third leading cause of death for 15- to 25-year-olds, and the sixth leading cause of death for 5- to 14-year-olds. How scary is that?

I didn't write this book to condemn working couples. You have to support your family. There are certainly ways that working parents can stay in touch with their kids, but there is no greater obligation than that. Still, parents have proven adept at insulating themselves from their difficult children and teens. One of the most popular methods is to drug their problem kids—and their kid's problems—out of their lives.

In the year 2000, doctors in the United States wrote almost 20 million prescriptions a month for Ritalin and simular stimulants—most of them for allegedly hyperactive children and teens. Those drugs had sales that year of $758 million, 13 percent more than in 1999. Drug companies now pitch this stuff as if it were just another home remedy, some sort of baby aspirin or castor oil. They run ads for it in *Ladies' Home Journal* and other "family" magazines.

What the ads don't make clear is that most of these drugs are Schedule II controlled substances. They are among the most addictive substances that are still legally sold. (Schedule I drugs, which are illegal, include heroin and LSD.) If you think kids aren't becoming addicted to this "prescription" stuff, think again. The federal Drug Enforcement Administration counts Ritalin and similar stimulants among the most frequently stolen prescription drugs. Across the country, teens have been crushing and snorting these pills to get a "Ritalin high."

We are all in a screaming dive here, and no one seems to have any idea what to do about it. Since the release of my first book, *Life Strategies for Teens,* I've traveled the country talking to parents and teens from Frisco to Philly and everywhere in-between. They talked to me and talked to me and talked to me. But they don't talk to each other.

We're going to fix that in this book. It's not an irreversible situation. There is hope. There is a way. Parents and teens are not incompatible. They are not two opposing forces in nature, except maybe when it comes to fighting over the remote to watch MTV versus PBS. My goal in this book is to show both parents and teens how to get what they want for themselves, for each other, and from each other. I'm going to show teens how to get more freedom, a better quality of life, and peace of mind. I'm going to show parents how to create an environment in which their teens can grow and flourish and make them proud.

I am going to show you practical methods and give you simple tools to work out your differences and disagreements. I'm going to help you turn those lose-lose negotiations into win-wins. You'll get what you want from each other because you're going to learn to focus on fulfilling *each other's* needs rather than just rying to get the other side to give in. You are no longer going to try to get things from someone else. You are going to meet *their* needs so that they will meet *your* needs. My dad is so good at this type of negotiating that other people ask him to negotiate their car deals and court settlements for them. "If you want what you want when you want it," he says, "meet the needs of the people on the other side."

So, teens: if you want your parents to do what you want, all you have to do is figure out what their needs are and meet them. I'll help you determine what their needs are in a later chapter, but as an example, one of your parents' greatest needs is *to know that you are safe.* They want to feel confident that even when they are not around, you are not in danger. That's reasonable. But how can you fill that need for them when they aren't around? By letting them know through your words and deeds that you have adopted their models of what is safe and what isn't.

As soon as you start reading this book, your relationship with your parents or with your teenager is going to start improving. There is only one requirement: You are going to have to work together. You are going to have to learn to see through each other's eyes.

Teens: If you want something from your parents, you won't get it by rebelling. You will get it as soon as you start talking to your parents and not a minute sooner.

Parents: If you want something from your teen, you won't get it by being a totalitarian dictator. Communication and mutual participation are the key. So turn off the television, unplug the earphones, and start working on forming a bond as a family.

The cool thing is that either one of you can start making huge improvements in your relationship even if your teen or your parent isn't reading this book along with you. You have the power to influence the relationship on your own. You make up half of it. The other half has to respond to everything you do. You might be surprised. He or she might just be waiting to see a sign that you will meet him or her halfway. If you start doing things differently, he or she will respond to you in a different manner. It may be easier if you go through the steps together, but the important thing is to get started—on your own or together.

By the time you've completed this book, you will be amazed at how much power and control you've created in your life. That's no bull; it's true. I know because I learned the principles and methods from my dad, who has been using them for a long, long, *long* time (don't worry, Dad, I'm not trying to suggest that you are really old or anything) in his work as a relationship and life strategies counselor. He used all this stuff on me, and I have to admit, it worked pretty darn well. We have always talked about everything. We've always worked things out. We are best friends. And we love and respect each other more than I can express—even when we simply agree to disagree.

My primary goal is to reconnect teens and parents. This book is

23

written from a young person's perspective, but with the benefit of my father's wisdom and training. One of the main messages I'll be delivering throughout this book may shock both teens and parents. It is contained in the story I told you at the beginning of this chapter.

Parents: If you think you are doing your kids a favor by telling them everything that they want to hear and believing everything they tell you, you are dead wrong. If you swallow their BS day after day, night after night, they will have no respect for you and they will very likely get into one huge mess after another to make that point.

Teens: I watched my friends defy and disrespect their clueless parents, and we both know that we want nothing more than for our parents to be strong enough to require things of us. We all know that when our parents buy into our BS we smile on the outside but we are seriously let down on the inside, wanting nothing more than for them to care enough to make us do our homework or be home on time. Let me tell you, there is a huge disconnect between parents and teens everywhere. MTV might as well be declared the legal guardian of two-thirds of the teens in America. Most teens spend more time with Kid Rock and Li'l Kim than Mom and Dad. Most teens know more about Tomb Raider and Britney Spears than they do about their parents. I would bet that if you stopped ten teens at the mall, more of them would know the birth date of some actor or musician than would know their parents' birthdays.

And most parents know more about what problems their favorite character on *The West Wing* are facing than their own teen's problems at school. Most parents know more about the state of their 401(k)s than their kid's classes, teammates, or best friends. Most parents spend more time working on their waistline than the relationship they have with their teens. Both sides pay a terrible price for this disconnection. Luckily, there is a deceptively simple way to hook families back up.

Did you know that the number one predictor of a troubled teen has nothing to do with parenting style or approach? It has nothing to do with whether or not the teen comes from a single-parent family or a double-income home. Nothing to do with the quality of the neighborhood or the family's ethnic background. None of that matters as much as the number one most important factor in your child's home life: *the number of words spoken*!!

Yep. The greatest things you can give your son or daughter are your ear and your voice. Listening and talking to your teen will save you more heartbreak than anything else a parent can do. You constantly hear cliché explanations for why teens get into trouble: "He's the product of a broken home" or "She just couldn't handle the peer pressure." Those things may contribute to the problem, but nothing influences the direction of young people's lives more than the quality of communication with their parents. Just talking? I know it sounds wild. How can that make a difference? Let me explain: in a house where there is no communication, there is no understanding.

Teen: "Mom, can I get a tattoo?"

Parent: "No."

End of discussion. But does it end the teen's desire to join a widespread fashion trend? Does it give the teen any understanding of his parent's reasoning? More important, does it give the teen any foundation for making his own decisions about similar matters in the future? No.

But what happens when a parent takes the time to discuss the reasoning behind a decision?

Teen: Mom, can I get a tattoo?

Parent: It's a fad. Fads die out. Tattoos don't. Will you still want it when you're my age? What do you think when you see an older person with tattoos? My answer is no, and I think if you honestly look at it as a long-term thing, you'll feel the same way.

Teens can learn how to reason things through if you give them a lead to follow. Look, we aren't Neanderthals. We know that sometimes we have hare-brained ideas just like our parents. (Do I need to give examples here? Does the term "streaking" mean anything to you, parents? Goldfish swallowing? Nehru jackets?) Parents don't do them-

25

selves or their teens any favors when they forget what it was like to be on the other side of the MTV-PBS line. When parents just say "No," they shut down lines of communication and they miss an opportunity to convey their belief systems to their teens.

Teens and parents do a great service to themselves and each other when they build a case based on logic and mature reasoning rather than command and control or righteous indignation. Teens are more thoughtful than parents often acknowledge. And just as you want to be proud of us, we want to make you proud.

The more you invest in your teens and your family—the more energy, the more words, the more emotion, and the more time—the more we respond. It works both ways, of course. If you're a teenager and you want your parents to understand you and see things from your point of view, you have to build a case—and that works only if you've built a relationship. Okay, I confess, I'm talking about bonding here. The real thing. Not the *Saturday Night Live* version. Not the kiss-kiss. Not the "quality time" hug-and-run. I'm not talking about becoming "let's do lunch" best friends here. Some of you may be starting from scratch. Some may need just a minor tune-up. Don't worry, either way, I'm going to give you a lot of tools and a lot of step-by-step instructions. Heck, we may even have a few laughs together. Wouldn't that be nice for a change?

In the chapters that follow, you will start to understand how you got disconnected from each other in the first place. Then I'm going to give you tools for coming to grips with the gaps in your relationship and in your understanding of each other. You've heard of urban myths? We'll look at Parent Myths and Teen Myths, the weird things you believe about each other even though they are no more true than that tall tale about a scalpel-wielding Body Parts Gang that drugs tourists and swipes their kidneys.

I'm also going to help you see how those parent-teen myths or misconceptions lead to behaviors that contaminate your relationship with each other. I'll offer insights into parents who push their teens away by always keeping score, finding fault, laying blame, or arguing about everything but the real issues. We're also going to take a look at teens who poison their relationship with their parents by treating them as a lost cause, assuming they know more, sabotaging communication, and acting out of anger and insecurity.

Once I've explained the things parents and teens do to push each other away. I'll give you some guidelines and ground rules for dealing with each other and rebuilding your relationship. Since the disagreements between teens and parents are often so volatile, I've included a really useful chapter on anger management that may save the hinges on all the doors in your house. Then we'll roll into my satisfaction-guaranteed, no-money-down, time-tested formula for reconnecting with your parents or your teens. It's sharper than the Ginsu Knife, hotter than the Ronco Showtime Rotisserie, and builds quicker than the Ab Roller!

We'll identify the most basic, and most important, needs of parents and teens, show you how to identify each other's needs, and then teach you how to make your needs known and how to meet each other's needs in ways that bring you together. I've even thrown in a letter that teens can give to their parents. It gives you license to talk to each other out of mutual respect rather than anger or hurt.

Finally, I've outlined an action plan that will provide you with natural, free-range, painless methods for getting back on track with each other. It's a tool, and you are free to use it any way you want.

The important thing is that you get moving right away, if not sooner. Think again to those parents who brought their beaten and battered 25-year-old daughter to my dad's seminar. Those parents wish they could go back and start over again. Their daughter wishes she had another chance too. But they can't go back. They've lost their opportunity to reconnect as parents and teen. You haven't. You still have a chance. Don't let your relationship end up like theirs. Don't let someone you love slip away. You owe it to yourself and to each other to give it your best shot. You get this chance only once. Then it's gone.

Let's get rocking. We're burning up important family time here.

2

THE WAKE-UP CALL

At 4 A.M. on a Saturday, John got the telephone call that all parents dread. It was a deputy sheriff asking him to come to the county jail. His 17-year-old son, Casey, and Casey's girlfriend had been in an accident. Casey was not hurt, but he was charged with drunken driving. His girl-friend had a mild concussion, and doctors had decided to keep her at the hospital overnight. At the jail, the desk sergeant told John that he'd need to pay $500 to bail Casey out.

As he filled out the forms and wrote the check, he grew angry. "I don't understand him! I gave him a good car because he promised he would be careful! Now he goes out and nearly kills himself and that girl. What's her name, anyway? Julie? Jane? What was he thinking? How do you control them, Sergeant?"

The deputy had heard this all a hundred times before. He knew that this father, like so many others, was angry and frustrated. And he knew that his advice would probably, once again, be disregarded. But he felt that this father needed a reality check. "You don't even know the full name of the girl he was with, do you? I'll bet you don't know anything about her parents or her background either. That tells me something, sir. It tells me that instead of buying your son another car, you might try sitting on your wallet instead of shoving it in his face. Turn off the damn television and talk to the boy. If you didn't see this coming, you weren't paying attention. I see him every weekend—different name, same deal!"

John knew the deputy was trying to open his eyes, but he was being judgmental and the words stung. "I give that boy as much time as I can, but I have to travel for my job. It's not easy supporting a family and keeping track of these teenagers too," he said as he handed over the check.

The desk sergeant accepted the bail bond payment and shrugged his shoulders. "I know it's tough, but when you don't know your son any better than that, this is the only type of *bond* you'll ever share with him. You'd better figure it out."

Falling into the Gap

The first step in fixing a problem is to acknowledge that it exists. So I want to help you clearly understand how I see the environment in which today's parents and teens live. Without a doubt, I have to tell you we are in the time of the greatest family crisis in the history of our country. The American family as portrayed on *Ozzie and Harriett, The Cosby Show,* and even *Family Ties* has gone the way of the eight-track tape, the Captain and Tennille, and the twenty-five-cent pay phone.

How did we get to this point? Dual-income parents. Divorce. Single mothers. Nobody is saying that they are all bad parents or bad people. It's just that when there is only one adult in the house only part of the day, kids get less face time with the most important influence in their lives, a parent. Less time means less interaction, less communication, less supervision, less modeling of acceptable behaviors and actions.

Differing family types aren't the only factor causing the meltdown in families. Today's teens have not only a separate culture—one marked by body piercings, tattoos, and drooping denim—they also have separate lives. In the 1960s, teens and parents warred over the stereo, the television set, and the car keys. Today, even middle-class teens have their own stereos, televisions, and cars. Throw in a cell phone, a home computer with Internet access, and a couple of credit cards, and what do they need parents for?

That may be the point. Many parents are so darn busy, they'd prefer that their teens go their own way. I'm not trying to pass on the blame, but parents have to realize that we weren't born to be bad. We did not come out of the womb as hell-raising rebels. We didn't screw ourselves up without a lot of help—or lack of it. Like it or not, parents have to take responsibility for the state of today's teens. It is parents' job to keep us "in control" and out of trouble. But that's not happening.

We might as well be living with a bunch of strangers who have absolutely no authority over us. We don't know each other anymore, and that is a big problem. Teens are out of control, and something has to be done before more get hurt. Simply standing by and waiting for your teen to "grow out of it" won't cut it. Your teen might not get the chance to grow out of it. Fourteen kids at Columbine High School didn't. *You* don't plan to hurt your children. Teens don't plan to hurt their parents. The Columbine parents and teens didn't plan it either. But it happened. Teenagers are not easy to deal with much of the time. If the problem's not hormonal, it's attitudinal. That's the way it's always been. But never before have parents been able to disengage so easily. No longer do they have to watch the same television set, listen to the same stereo, and ride in the same car. Now we can stay quietly in our rooms and lose ourselves on the Internet for hours while instant-messaging friends, playing elaborate games with opponents on the other side of the world, or scrolling through one porn Web site after another. We are home, safe, and quiet. We are low maintenance. It's a weary parent's dream. And society's nightmare.

What's my evidence?

Exhibit A: Eric Harris secretly plants homemade bombs all over his school after threatening violence against classmates for months on his own Web site. Then he goes into Columbine High School with a friend armed to the teeth. In a matter of minutes, they kill twelve students and a teacher, then commit suicide. Harris's parents claimed they had no idea that Eric and his friend were building bombs, stockpiling weapons, and plotting one of the worst mass murders in history—in his bedroom.

Charles Ewing, the author of *When Children Kill,* has estimated that 60 to 70 percent of school shooters talked about their killings in advance. The warnings were put out, but nobody was listening. Teens are more isolated, more out of control, and in more danger than ever before, and all too often their parents are too busy to deal with their problems—if they even know what their problems are.

As much as I am trying to support and explain the plight of today's teens, I don't absolve them from all responsibility. If we don't like the way our parents treat us, we need to realize that we have a role in deciding what that treatment is going to be. We have to give our parents a reason to treat us the way we want to be treated. That is impossible if we don't even know them or communicate with them. You have to make the effort to get the reward even if you are just a teenager.

Think about when you first knew the person who became your best friend. It wasn't always so easy to share feelings, was it? Remember how you had to work your way into each other's trust and confidence? You didn't immediately take an interest in that person's life, did you? Now contrast that with your friendship today. You know, respect, talk to, and care about each other.

The relationships we have with our parents are no different. We have to get to know them, respect them, talk to them, and care about them, because when we do, they will do the same for us. Maybe it doesn't seem right that you should have to try to get to know your parents. But it beats the alternative, doesn't it? Sometimes it takes a little effort to get a big reward. Having a strong, trusting, and supportive relationship with a parent is one of those gifts that just keeps on giving. Nothing on the Internet can replace it. Nothing pays off more in the long run.

I'm only 22 years old, but I've reaped incredible benefits from my solid relationship with my parents. They've given me guidance and support and steered me clear of major pitfalls all of my life, but especially in recent years. What can parents give us or teach us after we've finished college and moved out? Oh, little things like how to negotiate for the best mortgage rate, or how to recognize when someone is abusing your trust, or what the wisest investments are. Your parents have life experiences and hard-earned wisdom that are invaluable assets as you begin your own adult life. And their love comes without a price tag if you are willing to invest a little effort in winning their trust and proving your own trustworthiness. Your family is the ultimate support network, but only if you've put as much into the relationship as you hope to take out.

I think some teens and parents give up on each other too easily. There seems to be an attitude that neither can be reached by the other. So everybody folds and walks away from the table without playing all the cards available. We now have so many distractions in our lives that we can go for days without ever speaking to each other. A mother recently told me that she and her son got into a huge argument about his reckless driving habits and didn't speak for almost three days. Finally her son asked where his baseball jersey was. Talk about your great icebreaker!

Not surprisingly, the mother went through the roof. She was frustrated that he finally spoke to her only when he needed something. Yet she was also sick to death of fighting all the time. She told him that he had really hurt her feelings by shutting her out.

"Mom, I thought we were just getting along," he said.

Not talking is *not* getting along. If you don't talk for the rest of your lives, does that mean that you've always gotten along? You don't talk to hundreds of strangers every day. Are you getting along with them too? If so, I've been getting along with Jennifer Lopez for years. Call the tabloids!

Parents and teens will always have some conflicts, just as every husband and wife have conflicts. But to have a relationship that will be a source of support and strength for a lifetime, you have to work through those conflicts by communicating. You can't communicate if you don't interact. In past decades, families had fewer options and distractions. They shared more time together. Today, we can get mad at our parents and go off to our rooms and surf the Net or watch one of seven hundred cable channels. That's the easiest way out, and we take it. We distract ourselves by diving into the bottomless well of self-entertainment. So we never deal with our problems. With each unresolved fight, we become a little more separated emotionally. Before we know it, there is a huge gap that we don't know how to reach across.

I know that you may be thinking, "Yeah, so what?" Let me ask you this: Do you have much influence over the family that lives down the street? Can you parents tell their kids when to be home at night? Can you teens take the neighbor's car to the movies? Of course not. You don't have any bond with those people. No interaction. No communication. You don't share anything with them other than a postal code.

If your parents don't know what makes you happy or sad or excited, if you don't care about their feelings or their happiness, there is no emotional bond between you. Is that what's happening within your family? It seems to be happening in a lot of them, according to the conversations I've had with parents and teens around the country. Here are a few examples of what I've been hearing.

- Mary is the mother of Matt, 13. "I just don't understand Matt anymore. He does some of the strangest things these days, and for no apparent reason. He is just changing so fast."
- Ashley, 17: "My parents are so boring, they won't let me do anything fun. And the TV shows they watch are so boring. My parents are kinda weird."
- Louis is the father of 15-year-old Megan. "Megan can almost drive, and I'm really worried about where she'll go when she gets her license. She has all new friends, and I don't know anything about any of them. I'm excited for her, but deep down I'm really scared that she'll hurt herself."
- Michael, 16: "I'm sick of my parents telling me what to do. I don't care if they *do* get mad, I'm going to do what I want to do and they can't stop me."

Maybe "reality" TV shows are so popular today because they truly are a mirror of how we live; a bunch of strangers sharing a house and walking circles around each other. It's great that you picked up this book because it shows that you know there are always ways to have a better relationship with your parents and your friends. Just how unplugged are you? I've put together questionnaires to help you determine just how much work you have ahead of you if you want to reconnect with the most important group of people in your life.

Below are two sets of questions, one for teens and one for parents. Answer the questions in your respective area. The questions address how much you know about each other. They can be answered with either "yes" or "no." Make sure you can truly answer each question if you are going to write "yes." Often people assume they know an answer, but when pressed, they really do not.

CONNECT THE PARENT QUESTIONNAIRE

Do you *really* know:

1. What your teen is putting most of his/her energy into right now?
2. What personal issues your teen is trying to resolve?
3. What daily hassles irritate your teen?
4. Who has the most daily influence on your teen's thoughts and behaviors?
5. The names of your teen's three closest friends?
6. Who your teen would confide in first if there were a serious problem?
7. What your teen considers to be his/her greatest strengths?
8. What your teen considers to be his/her greatest weaknesses?
9. Who your teen considers to be his/her biggest enemies?
10. Your teen's favorite time of day?
11. Your teen's favorite movies?
12. Your teen's favorite childhood stories?
13. Your teen's favorite hobby or pastime?
14. Your teen's favorite colors?
15. Your teen's favorite foods or meals?
16. Your teen's heroes?

35

17. Your teen's favorite song, band, or singer?
18. Your teen's favorite books?
19. Your teen's favorite television shows?
20. Your teen's attitude about his/her body?

CONNECT THE TEEN QUESTIONNAIRE

Do you *really* know:

1. What your parents are putting most of their energy into right now?
2. What personal problems your parents are trying to resolve?
3. What really irritates your parents?
4. Who has most influenced your parents' thoughts and behaviors?
5. The names of your parents' three best friends?
6. Who your parents go to first if they have a problem?
7. What your parents consider to be their greatest strengths?
8. What your parents think are their greatest weaknesses?
9. Who your parents' enemies are?
10. Your parents' favorite time of day?
11. Your parents' favorite movies?
12. Your parents' favorite childhood stories?
13. Your parents' favorite pastime or hobby?
14. Your parents' favorite colors?
15. Your parents' favorite foods or meals?
16. Who has inspired your parents the most?
17. Your parents' favorite songs, bands, or singers?
18. Your parents' favorite books?
19. Your parents' favorite television shows?
20. Your parents' health concerns?

If you could answer "yes" to every question in your section, you apparently have invested considerable time in getting to know your parent(s)/teen. If that's truly the case, you can skip the rest of this chapter—do not pass Go, do not collect $200—and go on to Chapter 3.

If you could not answer "yes" to every question, there's a gap between you and your parent(s)/teen. The more questions that stumped you, the bigger the gap. To mend your relationship and to vastly improve the quality of your lives, you will need to bridge that gap. Troubled and stressful family relationships contribute to all sorts of physical and mental problems, including depression, heart disease, and even cancer. Strong family relationships can get you through almost any crisis.

Are you willing to step up and do something about the disconnection in your family? Are you willing to take responsibility for developing a reconnection and building a healthy relationship? I warn you that this is going to take commitment and courage. But it will change your life.

Okay, let's get down to business. What does it take to close the gap? Keep in mind that people often exaggerate their feelings when they are stressed out about something. Sometimes we focus so much on negatives that we forget the positives in our lives. Often our problems so overwhelm us that we fail to see the solutions even when they're right there. The only thing worse than having a relationship that's in trouble is to have a relationship in trouble and not have the courage and commitment to change it.

Before we get started, I'd like you to answer five basic questions. These are questions for you and you only. Nobody else is going to know how you've answered them. To heal your parent-teen relationship, it is extremely important that both of you feel comfortable, or at least unthreatened, in each other's company. These five questions are designed to make certain that you feel safe with your teen or parent.

1. Do you want to make your parent(s)/teen feel more safe and secure?
2. Will you work at making sure that your parent(s)/teen never feel(s) unloved or unwanted?
3. Are you willing to let go of negative feelings and start fresh?

4. Is your current unhappiness with the relationship unacceptable?

5. Are you willing to work at making things better, rather than give up if things get difficult?

If you answered yes to all these questions, you're ready to move ahead. If you answered no, I guess you aren't ready to make a change yet. In some ways, I understand that. Change is a scary thing for many people. Even though you don't like the way your relationship with your teen or parent is now, at least you're familiar with it, right? Why risk ending up with something worse? If you're agreeing with me here, it's scary. That's exactly the kind of thinking that holds both men and women in self-destructive relationships that cripple their lives and, all too often, result in terrible abuse and even death.

That's dead-end thinking. It's brain-dead thinking too.

You don't get what you deserve. You get what you go after. If right now your relationship with your teen or your parents is not supportive, loving, understanding, and awesome for both of you, it should be and can be. I'm not going to say that you ought to be leaping into each other's arms every minute of every day, but it can be better. It can be what you are willing to make it. There's no reason to settle for a half-ass relationship. And there's every reason to think it can be better. Things can be changed for the better. People can change their ways if you give them reasons to do so.

I'm a pretty good example of that. I don't want to say that I was a poor student in high school, but I was voted most uninterested in all things academic! It was pretty ugly. If I wasn't in the gym playing basketball or in the locker room getting ready to play basketball, you can bet I was telling everybody how much I liked playing basketball. I had a rather limited vision of my life—a pretty ridiculous one too, since I don't exactly measure up to the NBA height requirements. I focused on basketball so much because I couldn't get my studies into focus at all.

I knew I wasn't stupid, but others weren't so convinced. High school was pretty much a wash for me as far as academics were concerned. I did not distinguish myself in my studies. My graduating class had a valedictorian, a salutatorian, and me, the stentorian (one who is proud to be loud). I did manage to get into a good college, though, and there something finally clicked. I began to take my studies seriously, and—wonder of wonders—I began to get good grades.

After a couple of years of college, I returned to my old high school feeling very much the Joe College smart guy. I don't know what I was thinking. I guess maybe I thought all my former teachers would recognize my newly installed intellect. Alas, they did not. They still treated me like the joking jock I'd been in my misspent youth. Their memories were so fixed and so rigid that they couldn't even imagine me as a good student, even though I really had changed. Let me tell you, that was *no* fun. By the time I got back in my car, they had almost convinced *me* that I was still a dumb jock.

They missed a chance to know the new, improved me. Don't you miss that opportunity with your parents or teens. Believe that people can change for the better. Believe that relationships can be changed with a few simple adjustments even by just one of the parties if the others are slow to grasp the opportunity.

If it helps you to do it this way, pretend for the rest of this book that your parents or your teens are totally new people whom you've never met before. You can establish a completely new relationship with each other. They really are going to be different people once you've changed your approach to your conflicts with them. They may have the same name and they may look the same, but they will be different because we are shaped in major ways by the relationships we have with each other. Your relationship with them is about to get *way* better, and when it does, you will become much closer.

3

TEEN MYTHS

The ancient Greeks didn't have the Weather Channel to explain thunderstorms, so they created the myth of Zeus, god of thunder and toga parties.

The Egyptian pharaohs felt that death was beneath them, so they dreamed up the myth of the Underworld, where mummies go to unwind.

Teens and parents often baffle each other. Neither can understand what the heck the other is trying to prove. So we've created myths to explain all the craziness that goes on between us. Those myths can really mess up both sides because myths by definition are untrue or, at the most, only partially true.

Today's teens and parents often don't interact enough to get to know each other beyond the myths and stereotypes. If both parents work and their teen is caught up in the daily rush of school, sports, clubs, activities, instant messaging, and just chillin' out, it's a wonder they even have time for disagreements and misunderstandings. But hot damn, they do!

It only makes things worse when both combatants go into the ring with all these parent-teen myths banging around in their heads and screwing up their perceptions. When you take a hard look at some of the myths that parents and teens have created about each other, they are beyond belief. We each have really screwy images of the other side. Teens see parents as alien life-forms that eat their young. Parents view teens as human fungi with attitude. Each side tends to exaggerate the flaws and failings of the other. Parents and teens are always accusing each other of having evil motives when, in truth, neither side has a dark agenda. Both are just trying to get through life without messing up.

To hear the myths we attribute to each other is like listening to some anthropologist interpret rap lyrics as serious social commentary. In fact, not long ago some highbrow cultural critic floated a four-alarm myth that rappers were attempting to establish a new world social order with their *subversive* lyrics. Maybe they do want a revolution. Or maybe they just want to hang out with naked babes in hot tubs!

But no matter how crazy or untrue they might be, myths can have a long shelf life. I'm sure there are still people in Greektown who pray to Zeus whenever a storm cloud rolls in. Every religion on the planet has its own version of the Egyptian Underworld, though some locate it higher than others. Superman and Conan the Barbarian are just updates on the Hercules myth. (Fabio too, before that whole bird-in-the-face thing happened.)

Some urban myths have been around for generations. There's the one about the teens who are out parking when they hear a radio report that a one-armed convict has escaped from a nearby prison. When they go home and get out of the car, they find his hook hand stuck on the car door handle. That one's been around since back when my dad was a chick magnet. For-*ever*. So has the one about the grandmother who secretly puts a little of her pee in her teenage grandson's orange juice to lower his testosterone count and mellow him out. I heard that one at my high school lunch table—the same place I learned that a girl can get pregnant by sitting on a dirty toilet seat, that masturbation will make hair grow on your palms, and that cigarette smoking is good for you because the tobacco tar coats your lungs.

Most myths are pretty harmless, but some that have been accepted as truth can mess us up. When we hang on to false perceptions too long, we unconsciously begin to form opinions based on them. The myths that dog the relationships of teens and parents are especially bad news. There is enough tension between us without throwing in un-truths and misperceptions. Some of the myths that teens believe about parents may originally have been created to explain our conflicts, but since they aren't really true they only make things worse. They get in the way of communication and understanding.

The myths surrounding teens and their parents are destructive be-cause they get brought out whenever there is an issue. They muddy things up and keep us from seeing each other more clearly. It's a damn shame. Because of these myths, you end up with teens who think all parents really are clueless control freaks. And you see mythed-up par-ents who assume that all teens are out-of-control party animals and junk-food junkies who have to be caged after midnight and force-fed green beans.

Bottom line: Our parent-teen relationships are infested with de-structive myths and we need to disarm them, take them out of the equation, and focus on the real issues. As your parent-teen ringside medic, I'm going to inject a little truth into those bad-boy myths and see if we can't clear up a few things. If this doesn't wipe them out, I'm bringing out the iodine and smelling salts, so pay attention.

Teen Myth No. 1:

43

My folks don't want me to have any fun.

At first this one seems to make sense. After all, our parents have always told us that when they were teens they walked six miles through snake-infested swamps just to get to their after-school jobs, which always seemed to involve hoisting one-ton blocks of ice onto horse-drawn wagons. They didn't have fun as teens, so why should we? Right?

Not right. This myth was created because of teen-parent conflicts that result from two classic conflicting needs: our need to have fun and their need to know that we are safe. It's probably true that our parents did a lot of dangerously nutty stuff when they were teenagers and that they're scared stiff that we'll try it too. But it's not that they don't want us to have fun. They just want us to be safe. That's not such an outrageous thing to want, is it?

Parents think we should limit our fun to sporting events, school sock hops (as if *those* are still happening), Disney-issue video games, swimming, casual dating, church socials, and hootenannies (don't ask). The typical parent is not at all enthusiastic about more exotic "fun" like drag racing, cow lipping, roof surfing, throwing eggs at cars, playing "chicken" on the freeway, ringing doorbells and running, smoking pot, or drinking alcohol until our eyes roll back into our heads.

I guess if you look at it through their eyes, it's understandable that they get a little nervous. They prefer risk-free fun for their little darlings. It's the nature of many teens to like at least a little danger with their fun. I'm sure there is a middle ground there. Maybe go-cart racing on a controlled track instead of drag racing on city streets? Throwing tomatoes at each other instead of at cars? Playing paint ball instead of chicken on the freeway?

When teens hold on to the antifun myth, it sabotages their efforts to get what they want from their parents. But if you try to understand their viewpoint, you might find a way to satisfy their need to know you are safe while fulfilling your need to have some fun.

Dumb Teen: "Dad, I want to go rock climbing with Charlie at Devil's Drop State Park. But I know you won't let me, right?"

Wise Teen: "I want to go rock climbing with Charlie. He's a certified climber and climbing trainer. He wants to teach me the basics on some easy rock walls just a few feet off the ground, and then we'll slowly work our way up. Don't worry, he has all the latest equipment, and he's a safety nut!"

Dumb Teen has swallowed the myth, and he's choking on it. Wise Teen has figured out what his parents' needs are, and he's made a strong case for doing what he wants to do because he's shown that he appreciates and understands those needs. Once you clear up the myth, it's all about communication and understanding.

Teen Myth No. 2:

My parents care only about what I do for them.

This myth holds that parents are looking for a payoff from their teens. A lot of parents say that no amount of payoff would be enough, considering all the annoyance we cost them. Get real. Unless you are Britney Spears or in sync with Justin Timberlake's take-home pay, odds are that as a teenager you aren't the primary source of the family income. It's really doubtful, then, that your earnings are important to your parents. Your parents may take an interest in other contributions you can make, such as cleaning the garage or taking out the garbage, but once again this myth is basically groundless. Teens aren't indentured servants. Nobody that I've ever met decides to have kids so that one day they'll have teens around to take care of chores and make life easy for the adult in the house. I think I can safely say that hasn't happened in America since the days of the horse-drawn plow.

Parents do take pride in our accomplishments. Some may go a little overboard and push us to the point of irritation over our performance in sports or in the classroom, but it rarely goes beyond parental pride. Some days we may feel like Cinderella or the errand boy, but parents have the right to expect us to chip in. If they take it too far, I'd suggest you get a copy of the child labor laws of your state and call in the feds. Otherwise, figure that all in all, your parents simply want you to understand that as you get older, you are expected to contribute more in the form of your time, energy, and ability to pick up day-old boxers off the bathroom floor.

Teen Myth No. 3:

My parents have no idea of what it is like to be a teenager.

Aw, c'mon. A lot of parents think they still *are* teenagers. How else do you explain all the blown Achilles tendons suffered by dads on the basketball and tennis courts and all the mothers with pierced navels and ankle tattoos? The reality is that most parents have way too many really *far-out* memories of their teenage years. That's why so many fathers want to frisk and interrogate their daughter's dates, and why so many mothers want to tear the eyeballs out of the guy guarding you in the state semifinals.

Nobody forgets what it is like to be a teenager because it's one of the most memorable times of life. That's why there are so many "coming of age" novels on the best-seller list. People want to relive those years.

So don't buy the myth that your parents are clueless about Teen World. The real problem might be that they are clueless about you and your life. If that's the case, it's up to you to clue them in. Get off the Net and spend some time with them. Let them know what's going on. If you haven't done this before, be patient. It'll take them a while to catch on that you are trying to get their attention. Try asking for their advice on a problem, but be careful, it may shock them into an irregular heartbeat. And if your dad or mom is getting on you about something, it may not hurt to ask them respectfully if they were ever in a similar position when *they* were teenagers. Warning: They may get overexcited and tell you about the time they almost went to Woodstock with six friends in a VW minivan with peace symbols on its hubcaps.

Teen Myth No. 4:

My parents control my life.

This myth doesn't hold water either. How many hours of the day do you actually spend with your parents watching over you? Maybe they control the car keys. Maybe they control the checking accounts and charge cards. But minute by minute, hour by hour, you make the decisions that guide your life. Sure, you don't have control over the world around you. None of us can control what happens to us, but we do control our responses.

This myth is a cop-out. It's an excuse for not taking responsibility. Your parents' role as major influences on your decisions is basically over by the time you leave junior high. After that, they mostly just watch from the cheap seats. That's a good thing because you have to try your wings.

The biggest factor in your success is how you perceive yourself and the decisions you make based on your self-confidence. If you see yourself as a loser, you will be a loser. If you see yourself as a victim, you will give up your control of your life. You have *total* control of your attitude and your responses to the things that life hurls at you. Your parents may seem as if they're trying to grab the wheel. But that's because they're scared for you. They want to help, and sometimes, it's true, they screw you up.

Give them credit for caring. Give yourself the gift of setting meaningful goals and going after them. Your parents' vision is probably much different, but if they are wise, they will be supportive if you decide to be all you can be—whatever that might be. The story of your life is yours to write, but only if you pick up the pen.

47

Teen Myth No. 5:

My parents don't want me to grow up.

It's true that sometimes parents get locked in a time warp. They may not want to acknowledge that their daughters and sons have become young adults because it means their offspring will soon be bolting the nest. Then they'd have to face spending less time in the laundry room or at those exciting school awards banquets!

If your mom still wants to dress you like one of the Brady Bunch, it's time for you to step up and teach your parents how to treat you. That's your responsibility, not theirs.

They want you to make reasonable decisions and to be accountable for your actions. How do they know you're ready to take the controls? You have to show them in ways that, once again, assure them that you are not going to put yourself at risk. They can't help it. They love your sorry butt.

Your parents do want you to grow up. In fact, it would thrill them to know that you are growing up and thriving on your own terms. But if you tend to date bozos, bang the Buick into immovable objects, and repeatedly run up the credit cards because you forget to pay them off, you can probably expect them to keep the *Pokémon* wallpaper up in your bedroom.

Your parents will treat you according to how you act. How many times have you heard "If you act like an adult, we will treat you like an adult; if you want to act like a child, we will treat you like a child"? If you are still refusing to eat your beets or still asking your mom to take the pickles off your Whopper, they might be tempted to think that you're not ready for your own apartment. But if you take responsibility for your life and let them know that you can think ahead further than the next commercial, they will probably bite the bullet and take the child safety seat out of the backseat of the Caravan.

To counter the effects of this myth, show them your maturity by telling them what your needs are and how you can meet some of theirs.

This is not a thirty-minute fix. You cannot go in and lay out your plan for the next four years and then expect an immediate stamp of approval and a small up-front loan.

Show them. I know a myth-busting teen who went to his parents at the age of 15 and described in detail each goal he was going to achieve, each challenge that would arise, how he would handle it, and his methods of dealing with any issues of personal safety. He followed through on each step through high school. He's now in medical school and on target to get his M.D.

Granted, this guy has hyperspeed DNA. He was grown up when he was twelve, and he may hit the wall at 40. I come from the slow-growth forest. I had to go at it one step at a time, but the principle is the same: give them a plan of how you are going to grow up, keep them informed, let them know you look both ways before crossing the street, and they'll give you the green light.

Teen Myth No. 6:

My parents will never change.

Is it the REO Speedwagon poster and the Grateful Dead autographed album cover in the rec room that make you accept this myth? The love beads your father wears to Rotary Club lunches? Your mother's go-go boots? Unless your parents are still spoon-feeding you Gerber pea slop, you can probably toss this myth in the Dumpster too.

Your parents will change as you change. It's a law of nature, the famous "It Takes Two to Tango Theorem." My dad has it tattooed on his forehead, along with the first three chapters of *War and Peace*. If your parents are guilty of loving you so much that they don't want to see you grow up and go away, well, there are worse sins. And it's not an incurable affliction. You simply have to demonstrate that you are ready to take responsibility for your life and move on.

Let them know that they've done their job: Don't put red clothes in with whites. Operate the microwave and the minivac without causing mass destruction.

Your parents want to change. They need to change so that they can go on with their lives and move to a gated community for denture wearers. They really do want to spend the rest of their lives not having to worry about being bad examples. So go ahead and grow up. They won't resent it, especially if you start paying for your own gas.

Teen Myth No. 7:

My parents never forget my screw-ups.

Okay, so you backed your dad's company car into your mom's company van. It was in your blind spot. And squirling Liquid Wrench instead of Spray Butter on your grandma's toast wasn't that big a deal. The containers looked exactly the same—except for the color and shape.

It seems that parents never forget anything, especially the times you screw up. Does this mean they'll never forgive you or give you any credit? Good news there. Scientists now report that there is a chemical in our brains that makes us forget pain. This chemical, which has a name longer than the Constitution, is abundant in the brains of women. It helps them forget the agony of childbirth. In males, it erases all memory of where they put the car keys. It's believed it may also help parents forgive their teens for setting the couch on fire.

You are going to screw up. Your parents are going to go ballistic. It will eventually become only a dim memory. But in the interim, try to show your parents that you learned a lesson. Use their criticisms to motivate yourself.

My girlfriend once jumped all over me because I used a male pig term for women. I was being an insensitive ass, and she shared that with me. Her words really stung, but she was right. I changed my attitude. I think this is called "sensitivity training."

Parents tend to keep the bad stuff in their minds until you overwhelm them with good stuff. If someone whaps you in the forehead with a slapjack, it's human nature to feel that sting until more pleasant encounters wipe out that memory. It's up to you to displace those bad memories. It might help not to summon them up whenever storm clouds roll in. "You always bitch at me because I was late that one time." This is not a wise retort. By referencing it, you keep that memory open. If you want to banish a remembrance to the recycle bin, delete it from your vocabulary. And give your parents some pleasant memories to replace it.

Teen Myth No. 8:

My parents don't respect my opinions.

The general rule is that if you want to be heard and respected, you have to speak from your heart and from true knowledge. Don't toss out fragments of information or opinions gathered from MTV or Headline News. If you want to challenge your parents' opinions or their views on an issue, do your homework and wow them with your depth of knowledge. They'll have to pay attention then.

As with most myths, this one has some basis in reality. Parents do tend to write off your opinions if you toss them out half baked or poorly informed. Ask yourself: Am I really trying to share my thoughts with them, or am I just trying to get a reaction? If your parents have tuned you out, command their attention with true insights and dazzling debate points. You can get their attention with the power of your words and thoughts. You don't have to hit them with a mallet. If talking to them doesn't work for you, try writing them a note from the heart. Since I am your full-service teen guru, I've composed an example:

"Dear Mom and Dad, I need you to listen and respect my opinions and views so that I can figure out my place in the world. I promise to respect your opinions if you treat me the same way. I want more of your time. I want us to understand each other. Let's sit down and figure out how we can meet each other's needs. I feel that we have only a little time left before I'm on my own. I want to make the most of it."

51

Teen Myth No. 9:

My parents think they know everything.

Ninety-nine percent of parents with teenagers confess to feeling dazed and confused about how to deal with them. Most claim that their kids grew up so fast that one day it just seemed as if a surly stranger came out of the bedroom. They feel unprepared. Dumbfounded. And out of control. Hard to figure where "know it all" fits into that equation. Maybe your parents are putting up a front to hide their insecurity and befuddlement. Gee, that would make them human, wouldn't it?

When parents try to come across as all-knowing and all-seeing, it is generally a defense mechanism, but it is also a counteroffensive be- cause—I know this is going to shock you—they sometimes feel that their teens treat them like irrelevant, pea-brained dinosaurs.

Brontosauruses have feelings too. You need to be sensitive to their insecurities. Show some respect for the wisdom of the ancients, and they just might admit that you have some potential.

Parents often lack a teen-handling gene. It's genetic. In my teen years I ran across one adult who seemed to have mutated. She was cool with teens. She was a high school counselor and the mother of a friend of mine. It wasn't that she was a pushover either. She had a finely tuned BS detector, but she didn't play "Gotcha." She'd just tell her son to knock it off. She always seemed to be one step ahead of any teen she encountered, but she didn't lord it over you. She didn't get mad. She didn't give lectures. She treated us like adults-in-training rather than overgrown kids.

One of the things that worked for her was that she always ex- plained her thought processes and motives. She was big on telling her son that her primary concern was his safety and well-being, and if he could satisfy that concern, he got the green light. She understood that his nature was to want to explore things, but it was her nature to make sure he didn't walk off a cliff. She taught me that the best approach to teens is to level with them instead of barking at them.

There are other myths that I hear every day, and I'm sure you have a few that I haven't listed here. I hope that reading these has at least inspired you to challenge the myths that you carry around about your parents. The same goes for the myths that you've created for yourself, like "I'm never going to be any good at math" or "I'll never have a date." Challenge all the myths that hold you back. Things change. You change. Give yourself—and your parents—the opportunity to grow.

4

PARENT MYTHS

Parents, I hope you read the previous chapter on Teen Myths because as a young person I have given you a behind-the-scenes look at how we think and feel about the relationship that we have with you. Reading the Teen Myths will help you understand your teen's perceptions and point of view about you and your relationship. Now it's your turn to be drilled. You are just as guilty of mythmaking as your teens. Think about the conversations you have about teenagers with other parents. Admit it, you recite all the stereotypical laments and myths: Your teens are defiant. They're self-centered. They'll dream up ingenious ways to do anything but what you want them to do. They're pod people stuffed with raging hormones!

You too have allowed certain myths to cloud your vision and affect your attitude toward your teens, which will prevent you from achieving success. In doing so, you have set your teens up for failure and contaminated your relationship. It's bad enough to write off your teens by accepting these myths; many parents make matters worse by setting unreasonable expectations for them. The best way to absolutely *ruin* your relationship with your teen is to set standards he or she can't reach or demand things he or she will never do. That's one bloody footstep into *Nightmare on* . . . (insert your street name here).

If you expect your teen to be perfectly behaved at home, in school, and at the local hangout, you're setting yourself up for disappointment. But if you expect that your relationship is going to be nothing more than snarling exchanges and stony silence, you've set the bar too low. So before we go any further, let me clear up some of the biggest myths and misconceptions parents have about their teens.

Parent Myth No. 1:

I can't be a friend to my teen.

This myth is a double-headed monster. I want to chop both heads off. Some parents believe the myth that they can't be both a friend and a disciplinarian. Others buy into the myth that they don't have a solid relationship with their teen unless they are buddies who never question their teen's actions.

No. No. Double no!

First, the fear-of-friendship myth: I have heard many parents say that they can't treat their teens as friends—or in a more relaxed manner—because it only confuses them and tempts them to be less respectful. As in the case of most myths, this one has a vein of truth mixed in with all of the bad information and misconceptions. It is difficult to be a friend and a parent at the same time. But that doesn't mean you can't do it.

Many parents mistakenly believe that they have to run their households like a boot camp for delinquent teens. It didn't work for The Great Santini, and it won't work for you. When you become Master Sergeants Dad and Mom, you destroy any emotional connection. Teens need that connection, even when they don't admit it. And so do you. So lose the camouflaged jumpsuit and steel-toed boots; they're just not necessary. Think about the authority figures you respected as a teen. They wielded their power firmly, fairly, consistently, and with good humor. They made the rules clear. They made the penalties or consequences equally clear. But they also showed that they could be understanding and forgiving. They may not have been "friends" like your high school pals, but they were friends in the sense that they had your best interests in mind and were interested in you without being judgmental. You can be firm without being mean, and you can be forgiving without being a pushover. That's all we want, and to think that it's not possible is seriously cheating your relationship.

And now the "buddies" myth: Sure, it's great when parents and teens feel that they're buddies. But both the parents and teens have to handle that sort of relationship with more maturity than usually comes in this sort of deal. Sooner or later, that buddy-to-buddy relationship is going to be tested. Will a teen be mature enough to understand that a parent's first duty is to be a guide, not a companion? Will the parent have the courage to risk the buddy relationship to save the teen?

Doing anything less would be cheating your teen. We enjoy your friendship, but we depend on you to be our parents. We look to you for direction, stability, and support, and those are things our friends are not able to give us. Realize that we do want to feel comfortable spending time with you. Know that you can see us as friends. But be aware that things can get awkward when a teen depends on his parents to be buddies too. The way we see it—although we would never admit it—is that we have a bunch of friends but only one or two parents. Don't cheat us out of having parents because you think we need a couple more friends. That is not at all what we want.

Can your daughter come to you as a "sistah" and tell you that she had a frightening experience on a date? Is it possible for you to respond to that as a buddy rather than as a parent? I doubt it. So if your child has neglected building friendships with her peers because "my mom is my best pal," where can she go to talk through such an experience and decide whether it merits serious action or not?

It must be entirely clear to you and your teen that you are a parent first and a buddy second. It is your responsibility. Have the guts to stand up and say "No" or to create negative consequences for irresponsible or dangerous behaviors. Your first role is to protect your child. Sometimes that puts you in the role of enforcing the rules. Can you be both the Enforcer and the Buddy?

Best buddies don't ground each other for missing curfew. That's where things get tricky. If you threaten a punishment and don't follow through, you cheat both sides. But if you are inflexible and unforgiving, you will shut down communication and understanding. No relationship or friendship can withstand that. Make rules. Enforce them. But be flexible and open. All I am saying is that it is OK to be friends, but you are required to be parents. That's the first priority. Besides, I can tell you that we will like and respect you far more for being a reasonable, predictable parent than we will for your being cool and fun to be around.

I heard a story recently about a prominent Hollywood director who told his 13-year-old daughter that if she got an A in math, he would give her a small part in a summer blockbuster he was working on. She hunkered down and worked like he'd never seen her work. But when the report cards came out, she'd gotten a B-plus instead of an A.

Her director dad didn't kick her out of the movie. He just gave her a smaller part than she'd hoped for. He gave her a B-plus part instead of an A part. And he told her that if she made the grade next time, he'd find her a better role in his next movie.

He was fair with her. That's all it takes to prove that you're both a parent and a friend. Most parents don't get to cast a blockbuster movie. But you do control the curfew time and the car keys. If your teen wants to see a movie that doesn't end until ten minutes after his usual curfew, it won't hurt to give him a little extra time.

But let your teens know that the rules become flexible only when they demonstrate trustworthiness, self-discipline, and reliability. Trust has to be earned. Parenting is a system of rewards and punishments, and it works only if you hand both out fairly and consistently.

Teens will do more for you out of respect than out of fear. As a son with a lot of friends who feel the same way about their parents, I promise you that I'd rather have a son or daughter thinking "I don't want to disappoint my dad" than "I could get my butt kicked for doing that."

It isn't easy to hardwire us with that sort of inner dialogue, but in the next few chapters I'm going to give you the tools to do so. First, though, you'll have to clear out the myths that cloud your vision of that young person across the breakfast counter.

Bottom line: It is a myth, a destructive myth, to hold to the belief that friendship between parent and teen is impossible. It's not an easy thing to pull off, and it isn't as important to be a friend as it is to be a consistent source of support and guidance. Friendship involves investing in the success of another person. A relationship based on anything else is dangerously limited and doesn't nurture either participant.

Nobody wants to be dominated or dictated to. We all want to know the "whys" behind rules and regulations. Set boundaries, but don't draw lines in the sand. On the other hand, don't dictate. Explain. Until you do all those things, you will never be a true friend to your teen.

Parent Myth No. 2:

A good relationship is a peaceful one.

I blame the '60s for this manic myth. It's a hippie hangover. Peace, brother. Give peace a chance. Peace, love, dope. People *peaced* all over themselves back then, and four decades later a whole lot of parents are still profligate peaceniks. It's Gandhi gone amok.

Peace and quiet have their place. The library comes to mind. Most of North Dakota. But peace and quiet are not valid indicators of a good relationship. Some peace and quiet is a good thing. Too much peace and quiet is the calm before the storm. Mount Saint Helens before the big blow.

Many parents are so nonconfrontational that they never give their teens boundaries or guidelines. How's a kid supposed to handle that? What will your teen do when she enters the messy, loud, confrontational real world? I had a friend who was a great athlete. He got a basketball scholarship to a major school. He lasted about a week, then quit the team and transferred. He ran into a head coach out of the Bobby Knight school. This coach believed that if he played the bellowing bad-cop role, his players would pull together as a team and elevate their

59

game. My buddy had always been a star at home and at school. His parents and coaches had coddled him because he was a good kid and extremely talented. But the first time he ran into a confrontational environment, he bailed out. He later ran into one of his former teammates, a guy who seemed to take the coach's rantings and insults in stride. He asked the other player how he could handle it.

"Hell, Coach never called me anything that my mother hadn't said a hundred times before," the teammate said. "I learned early on that you have to listen to the message, not the words."

I don't advocate screaming or cursing at your teens. That's not necessary. But you can't abandon your responsibilities as a parent just for the sake of keeping the peace. That's not peace. It's neglect.

Peace isn't an environmental issue. It's a mental health issue. It exists inside you. Parents who say that they want a peaceful relationship with their teens are looking for a free ride. But I can guaran-damn-tee you that they'll pay a price sooner or later. Or their teen will.

You have to stand in harm's way. You have to risk being the bad guy to give your teen the guidance he needs. Be willing to argue to get your teen to do what is right. A lot of times we don't know something and you do; have the guts to tell us about it. Just because we argue occasionally does not mean that we don't respect each other. It doesn't mean that we don't like each other. It doesn't mean that we can't find some resolution to our problems. Silence is cowardice. Every relationship is marked by differences of opinion and conflicting viewpoints.

You can disrupt the peace without destroying a relationship. It is OK to argue, even better to negotiate. There are very few situations that cannot be resolved. Don't ever be scared to try and resolve your disputes. When you make the effort to resolve conflicts, you clear the air and make boundaries more clear. And sometimes it's perfectly okay to shake hands and agree to disagree.

Bottom line: Don't be afraid to argue. You don't want anyone in your house to explode, so make sure some of the pressure gets released. But be careful to realize the difference between fighting and arguing.

Parent Myth No. 3:

Once a bad kid, always a bad kid.
Once a good kid, always a good kid.

Kim, a high school sophomore and cheerleader, was caught drinking at a huge party at a friend's house. Her parents were rightfully upset, and they disciplined her when they learned of it. But they haven't stopped. She is still getting twenty-minute lectures on the evils of alcohol, and they are constantly reminding her that she disappointed them that night.

Now, I confess, Kim should not have been drinking at that age. Her parents were right to discipline her. But that was eleven years ago. Yes, Kim is now 27 years old, married, and living with her husband two thousand miles from her parents. She just picked up her master's degree in business. But still, every year when she (and her *husband*) come home for Christmas, Kim's parents lecture her about her "drinking." It is as if that is all they can remember.

She is a fully self-sufficient adult, but her parents still haven't gotten over the fact that she got caught with a Heineken in hand at a friend's beer bash when she was 16. She's stuck with a life sentence when she should have been paroled a long time ago. Kim's parents need to get over their teen's lapse in judgment. Do you?

This myth has caused a lot of damage. And it's such a load of bull. Did you make the same mistakes at 18 that you made at 14? I don't think so. Do you make the same mistakes at 37 that you did at 17? Probably not, because you and your maturity level have changed. You make entirely new and fresh mistakes with each passing year. It's human nature. Your teens have changed too, and they deserve a fresh chance. And it may sound weird, but you deserve a fresh chance as their parent too.

When you stick the "bad kid" label on a teen, you tell him or her, "Live down to my low expectations." We figure that we'll never con-

61

vince you that we've changed, so why bother? Why not play the bad-girl/bad-boy role? It worked for Madonna and James Dean.

It's no favor to label a kid a "good teen" or a "golden child" either, because sooner or later, we're gonna mess up about something. Even if it's a small slip, we're going to feel as if we ax-murdered a kindergarten class. The good boy gone bad—that's a heavy burden for a teen to carry.

I remember a mother who had two kids, a daughter and a son. Her daughter could do no right and her son could do no wrong, and the labels pasted on them early in life screwed up both. The daughter internalized her mother's criticism, and for a long time she was insecure and unhappy. The good son came to believe that he was truly a golden child. He had a hard time of it when his teachers, and later his bosses, criticized his work in any way. He had to make some serious adjustments in his attitude and face the reality that he wasn't perfect. You are tricking yourself and cheating your teens if you believe the myth that they don't change. Sometimes it's easier for parents to lie to themselves than to face reality. Parents shouldn't forget, but they need to forgive and they need to be realistic in their appraisals of their offspring.

If you don't give your teen the chance to regain your trust, you risk sliding into intolerance and command-and-control parenting, which is a sure formula for teenage rebellion. How many tongue studs would you like little Billy to have?

Condemnation is not a parental duty. You are not the hanging judge. Nor are you the Enforcer of Impossibly High Standards. (I think that was a Monty Python character.) You are a guide and a protector.

We all change. Respect that fact and reject the myth. Give us a chance to earn your trust back if we have lost it. And don't let the halo fool you; take us for what we are.

Bottom line: No one is the same forever. If you believe that, you are cheating someone, either your teen or yourself. Do not be so rigid that you refuse to see change in your teen.

Parent Myth No. 4:

No conflict is resolved until you and your teen see eye to eye.

This is one of the most deadly relationship myths. Parents who believe it are prone to spontaneous self-combustion.

In the environment created by this myth, the smallest disagreements can quickly deteriorate into major blowups that can last for days, weeks, months, even years. Phrases such as "Why can't you be more like me?" and "You'll come around to my way of thinking eventually" are early-warning signs that you have stepped on this land mine of a myth.

You and your teen have a lot in common. Build your relationship and friendship upon those things. And understand that you will always view some things differently, based on your different levels of experience. It is unrealistic and unfair to expect your teen to always do things, see things, or react to things just as you would.

Sometimes your teen will take a differing view just to prove she's not your puppet. You have to accept that—unless, of course, you enjoy bashing your head against a brick wall. You can't force your opinions and views on your teen. "You should do it because I am your mother and I said you should do it" may be classic parent patois, but it is not what a sales technique expert would call a great "closer." It gets you nowhere in Teen Town.

This is real life, and you have to take a realistic approach to it. Quit telling yourself that everything is going to work itself out. It won't. Your disputes with your teens aren't splinters. They are barbed treble-hooks. Once they get under your skin, they stay there unless you take healing action.

It's myth-tifying to me that anyone would buy this one. How can a parent reasonably expect a teen to see things through the same eyes? Parents have taxes, house payments, high blood pressure, jobs, and

63

aches in body parts the kid hasn't even located yet. Teens have home-work, sports, peer pressure, MTV, screen names, and the ability to eat 60,000 calories a day while maintaining the waistline of a soldier ant.

You are two different people in two different worlds. You and your teen are like lab rats conditioned to entirely different stimuli. One has to run around in the maze all day and ring the bell at the end of it. The other gets on and off the treadmill a couple times, naps, sleeps, and so-cializes with the rat pack.

You can't ever expect to, nor should you want to, see things through each other's eyes. Parents have "been there and done that," and teens are trying their best to experience "that" and have a good time along the way. Please understand: I am not telling you that you should not try to be compatible. We share many basic needs and prob-ably similar values, but our similarities are not going to create what we want in a connection. We have to learn how to be different philosoph-ically but connected emotionally. Parents may have different lifestyles, but they have the same feelings.

The key here is mutual respect. And having no fear. Some parents are fearful that if their kids aren't forced to see things their way, they will lose control. It doesn't have to be that way. Your teen might actu-ally respect you even more if you demonstrate that you respect his or her opinions but you have to live up to your parental responsibilities.

Here is a conversation likely to take place in any teen household.

Teen: Mom, Dad, can I stay out for an extra hour tonight?

M/D: We talked about this last weekend, and the answer is *still* no.

Teen: But please, everyone else gets to. I'm always the first person that has to come home, and it's embarrassing.

M/D: No.

Teen: That's not fair, I—

M/D: If you keep asking, I won't let you go out at all.

Teen: Fine. (stomps off)

This common disagreement between parents and teens will never be resolved because the parents' need to keep the teen safe is in direct conflict with the teen's need for greater freedom. Neither side sees any room to waffle. There is no need to waffle because you can leave some disagreements unresolved and still have a strong, healthy relationship.

The key is to get both sides to agree that they've reached an impasse because of two legitimate opinions. You must then agree that your emotional bonds are strong enough to handle your philosophical differences. It's OK to argue or debate, but it is important to do so in a way that does not resort to personal attacks or hostility. Disagree and debate over the issues, not each other's feelings.

Try this phrase on for size: "We can agree to disagree on this point." I'm telling you, it's magic. It stops the shouting. It eases migraines. It loosens up the shoulder muscles and takes the overheated emotions out of the teen-parent equation. Keep it. It's yours. A little bonus to yourself and your teen, with my compliments.

Bottom line: Decide to just accept that some things will never be resolved but it's OK. You can still get along.

65

Parent Myth No. 5:

Share everything with your teen.

Oh yeah, I smoked pot when I was your age. I did a bong every day before class with the other girls in my commune. Wow! But hey, things were different then. You need to stay away from that stuff.

Sure, your mother and I had sex before we got married. It was the '60s, dammit! But we were lucky. If I find out you're having sex, I'll lock you in your room until your first Social Security check arrives.

This absolutely idiotic myth holds that to bond with your teen you need to be honest and totally open about your own youthful indiscretions. Let's cut that in half.

Do be honest.

Don't be totally open.

Look, as a parent you have no duty to serve as a good example of a bad example. Stick with the good. Skip the bad. Hedge things if you have to.

Your teen will never admit it, but you are the primary role model and standard-bearer in his or her life. We operate under the theory that if Mom or Dad did it, it's OK for us to do it. You may have sat out the sexual revolution. Maybe you really didn't inhale. For all I know, you never fishtailed your dad's Grand Prix at ninety miles per hour while swigging from a fifth of Jack Daniel's. Good for you. Whatever happened back then, leave it. Anything short of making Eagle Scout or Betty Crocker Homemaker of the Year, keep it to yourself.

I'm not suggesting that you should lie to your teen about your tawdry past. Just don't bring it up. If your teen has questions that could lead into your trip across the Mexican border in 1972, put up a smoke screen: "Whaddya say we go do some test drives at the BMW dealership?"

Another thing that fits into this particular myth: you don't always have to say what's on your mind when addressing your teen. You can have a very good, very healthy relationship without getting absolutely everything off your chest. Better to stifle yourself than to regret it later. You can't unring a bell. One word can become a life sentence played out over and over again. If you have a problem with your teen, make your concerns known. But don't say things you will instantly regret. This is particularly true in the heat of an argument. If the temptation to do something hurtful comes, for your own sake, let it pass. Hurting never heals.

Remember, my brother, whatever be your goal.
Keep your eye on the doughnut, not on the hole.

Bottom line: Your goal is to connect with your teen. Connections are made through understanding and mutual support. There's no place for blaming, shaming, or condemning in that relationship. Be honest, but please don't volunteer everything. My dad has always told me, "Jay, never, ever miss a good chance to shut up." I pass that same scholarly wisdom on to you here.

Parent Myth No. 0:

You can fix your teen.

I'd like to open this final Parent Myth with a little song I call "The I Got a Wild Child and I Don't Know What to Do Parent of a Teenager Blues." It goes something like this:

> You can change the battery in your car.
> You can patch your roof with a little tar.
> You can scrub your windows to get 'em sparklin' clean!
> But baby, oh baby, there ain't no fixin' a messed-up teen!

Okay, so I won't quit my day job just yet. In fact, I'll make a deal with you, I promise that I won't waste my time trying to make it as a blues singer if you promise not to try to "fix" your teenager. My dad is always telling me about young people who make the mistake of thinking that all of their relationship problems will end once they "fix" their partner. Parents of teens make the same mistake when they buy into this myth. And baby, oh baby, it brings them nothin' but the blues.

You can't fix "messed-up" teens. If your relationship with them isn't working, you have to fix yourself instead. Nature isn't perfect. (Just look at the platypus. I mean, really, what is *that* all about?) Human nature has its failings too. One of the totally weird aspects of human nature that seems to plague parents—and couples too—is the tendency to blame everyone but yourself for your own unhappiness.

I've often heard parents say, "If my teenager would just change her attitude, we'd get along fine."

Changing a teen's attitude is not as easy as changing your car's oil. That's why you don't see Jiffy 'Tudes on every street corner. Believe me, the market is there, but the repairs are too complicated and the price is too steep. You can't fix people who refuse to accept that they've

67

got a problem. Teens are notorious for that. And you can't blame them because a lot of the "bad attitude" they put out is the result of chemical changes in their brains. I'll tell you more about that later, but take my word for it, teens are confusing because *they* are confused by all the changes they are going through. You have to let nature take its course to some degree.

So instead of trying to "fix" the teen in your life, I suggest you put your own attitude on the workbench and give it a tune-up. Are there things you could do to improve your relationship with your teen? Maybe your teen is out of control. But you are the adult. You should be able to evaluate the situation and find a way to reach this young person.

As the parent of a teen, you've been around awhile (I mean this in the best way possible). You've learned that you can't fix things that are forces of nature, like tornadoes, hurricanes, or floods. Instead, you adjust your activities to deal with them. You bring in the patio furniture, board up the windows, and head for a well-stocked shelter to wait it out.

Teens are a force of nature too. You can't fix them. You can only search for the best ways to deal with them. I'd suggest bringing in your ego. Boarding up your anger. And showering your teens with plentiful stores of patience, humor, and love. You may not be able to control your teen's emotional and volatile nature all the time, but you are 100 percent in control of how you respond to it.

We will test you. But you have all the advantages and wisdom of a mature adult at your disposal. You can find a way to reach out without pushing your teen away. It won't be easy, but fixing yourself first is a far better approach.

Bottom line: Don't try to fix *them;* its a waste of time. As Michael Jackson says, "Start with the man in the mirror."

Illogical Logic

Perhaps the biggest myth of all is that there is logic to relationships. Logic is a step-by-step system that derives conclusions from analysis, but human relationships defy logic. Relationships are based on emotional ties and personal history, which are circular and mysterious. There are few, if any, books that offer realistic answers to parent-teen relationships, especially from a teen's perspective. Many counselors are themselves the sources of ugly myths about teens and their parents. Some of these myth mind-sets may have been part of your belief system for a long time. You may have difficulty giving them up. But it is critical that you abandon them. Otherwise, you will continue to misdiagnose and mistreat your relationship with your teen.

5

PARENT POISONS

I've explained that parent and teen myths are false beliefs that sabotage our relationships by screwing up our perceptions of each other. When your perceptions are out of whack, you tend to take wrongheaded actions that only make things worse. These actions *poison* your relationship with your teenagers. They are the result of bad information, poor experience, poor skills, bad advice, and bad timing. In this chapter, I'm going to show you how to avoid these parent poisons. Teens should come along for the ride. You'll get insights into what goes on when the ugly head of stress clamps its fangs into Mom and Dad. You'll learn how to administer antivenom to counter the stress and show your parents how mature you are.

Parents, you need to recognize and understand the poisonous actions that commonly cripple parent-teen relationships. For the most part, you don't do them on purpose. Most are very human reactions to stressful situations. We all do irrational and destructive things when we are under stress. And to be straight up about it, sometimes even parents can be immature, selfish, controlling, and power hungry. You may not see it in yourself. Even if you do, no parent wants to admit that he or she might occasionally, sometimes, do things that are less than wise, just, and soaked with good intentions.

Just as you can send your relationships over the cliff by adhering to myths, you also have the capacity to poison them—and it takes only a split second to do it. Even a normal, intelligent, and caring parent can be capable of cruel and destructive behavior when confronted with a rebellious teen.

You ask your teen to do something. He ignores you. You ask again. He brushes you off or fires off a patented bit of teen 'tude.

Suddenly you feel your canines lengthen two inches and sharpen to a razor point. Claws appear at the end of your fingers. Scales ripple on your arms and legs. An unearthly roar bellows from deep in your chest, rattling the good china. Then it's Godzilla versus King Kong in the family room.

Yep, just when you think you've got it under control, your teen gives you an eye roll and a lame excuse and it's Rumble in the Jungle time. You go ballistic. Your teen realizes too late that he's pushed things beyond the limit. The parent-teen war enters a new phase that bloodies both sides. Anger. Frustration. The pot boils.

When it's over, you wonder how it got to that hurtful point. Naturally, you blame the teen for shoving you over the brink: "I may be reactive and out of control sometimes, but he pushes me too far. It's his fault. I'm not like this normally. It's teenagers. They're impossible to deal with."

A famous prosecutor once said that when we serve as our own judge, we tend to be very kind in our rulings. Sure, teens can try the patience of a saint, but you're the adult here. You knew the teenage years were coming up. You're supposed to be the one who handles this period with grace and wisdom. Instead, you did a meltdown. It's time to take an objective look at what has poisoned your ability to deal with your almost-adult child.

Some poisonous behaviors are quick and devastating. They end a parent-teen relationship in a matter of seconds. Others may act slowly. Their origins are based on your own experiences and emotional baggage. You may not be able to change what happened to you earlier in life, but it can be extremely helpful to consider whether things that happened to you as a teen are influencing the way you treat your own child at this stage. There's no shame in admitting that. No one is going to condemn you for wanting to shake the demons and make things better for your family. This is not the time to be defensive. You aren't the only parent to realize that your personal history may be influencing your behavior toward your teen.

Are painful or hurtful memories of your own youth poisoning your relationship with your teen? It's not too late to eliminate that poison and move on. The first step toward making a positive change is to acknowledge that you're unhappy with the way things are. To change the results you've been getting, you've got to change the way you've been acting.

Let's take a look at the most common poisonous behaviors for parents and the influences behind them.

Parent Poison No. 1:

Keeping score

It's tough to resist the temptation to track the goofiest things your teen does. And we do some really goofy things, I admit. But what purpose does it serve to keep score of the goofiness other than to demean the kid? When do you forgive and forget? When do you just write it off as a learning experience? When do you admit that, hey, you did some nutball things as a teen too?

Parents tend to remember a teen's screwups and to parade them whenever there is a disagreement, or sometimes just for the amusement of friends and relatives. It's not as if setting fire to the garage was an intentional act, or that it has any relevance to the teen's life. If the teen has proven that it was an accident and not the act of a dedicated pyromaniac, let it go. This scorekeeping is common between fathers and sons and between mothers and daughters. It seems to be a competitive thing. Maybe the parents instinctively fear that sooner or later the younger person will become stronger and more powerful. Maybe that threatens them.

Parents become used to sitting at the head of the table. They may even get a little power mad. It's intimidating for a father to see his son towering over him, flexing younger, stronger muscles—and maybe even a 4.0 grade point average too. It's just as intimidating for a mother to see her daughter blossoming into a younger, more attractive, and perhaps more intelligent female presence. It's not something you can prepare yourself for. It can be shocking to realize that your dependent child is becoming self-sufficient, confident, and, at the same time, less impressed with your power.

I had a friend in high school whose father, Greg, was obese. When his weight climbed to 380 pounds, Greg's doctor considered surgery to staple his stomach closed. The operation actually makes the stomach much smaller, so that less food can be consumed and absorbed by the body. It's a drastic measure, but it's proven effective where other methods have failed.

My friend Paul, Greg's son, was no lightweight himself. He weighed at least 200 pounds when he was 18 years old. This father and son had an odd and self-destructive relationship when it came to their bodies. Both of them seemed to take some sort of macho pride in their weight. They joked about it to a degree, but there was a competitive edge to their discussions of who could eat the most or who weighed the most. This competitiveness carried over into nearly every conversation, whether it was about their physiques, a football game, or whose turn it was to mow the lawn. Often their exchanges were funny, but sometimes they seemed to be baiting each other.

Prior to scheduling Greg's surgery, his doctor demanded that he first try an aggressive diet to get his weight down. "Before I put you on the operating table and cut you open, I want you to try this diet," the doctor said. "And I want you to push yourself to reach your ideal weight—210 pounds."

My friend's father looked at the doctor as if he'd just told him to lop off a limb.

When the physician asked him what was wrong with that target weight, he said that it was too low. So what would be a better goal? the doctor asked.

Immediately Greg said, "235 pounds."

"OK, why 235 pounds?" the doctor asked.

"Because that's how much my son is going to weigh when he stops growing, and I can't be *smaller* than my son!"

Big surprise: Greg never made his target weight. His bizarre score-keeping with his son convinced the doctor that Greg was not ready for surgery either. A few years later Paul could physically overpower his father, whose weight had increased to 400 pounds. But at that point the competition was over. Greg's heart condition was dangerous. Any physical strain was a threat to his life. So the son became the dominant male in the house. What did it prove?

Those poisonous behaviors cripple not only relationships but lives. Your connection with your teen should not be based on competition. That's a lose-lose game. A loving and mutually supportive relationship is not possible when both sides are fighting for leverage, power, or control.

Too often, when parents "keep score," it turns into a contest of who can inflict the most pain. Communication breaks down. Understanding is lost. You become adversaries and enemies rather than guides and helpers. There is no "winning" in this kind of parent-teen relationship. When one of you loses, you both lose.

Here are a few telltale signs that you can use to determine if you are poisoning your relationship by keeping score:

- You seldom let any mistake go without comment. If your teen says things such as "You'll never let me forget that one," you need to throw the score book into the fireplace.
- You demand psychic powers of your teen with phrases such as "You should have *known* I was worried. You should have *known* that I wanted you home for dinner. You should have *known* better."
- You unfairly employ exaggeration and overblown language to inflate your case against your teen: "You *always* forget your responsibilities" or "You *never* pay attention to me."
- When you have an argument with your teen, you find yourself going on the counterattack rather than using reasoning, self-control, and healing language.

75

- You demand that your teen admit defeat, confess to being wrong, and accept that she was irresponsible. Do you want her to take fifty lashes too? This is the ultimate form of poisonous competition and petty scorekeeping. Don't do it!

Keeping score won't make your teen a better person. It may make the teen more cunning and crafty and a better game player, but those aren't generally considered useful. They're antisocial behaviors that will lead your child to poison future relationships. Is that what you want? It's far better to honor your teen by building his confidence than to condemn him and teach him that relationships are a form of competition rather than a gift to be respected and cultivated.

Parent Poison No. 2:

Finding fault

Do you enjoy being told that you're screwing up your child? How does it feel to have some wise guy tell you that you don't have a clue about how to be a good parent to your teen? What's it like to realize you don't know it all, smart guy?

The really poisonous thing about faultfinding is that when a teen hears time and time again that she is a screwup, she begins to accept it as her nature. You have that kind of power over your teenagers, whether they acknowledge it or not.

Teens may act as if they are ignoring you, but they internalize the things you say about them. If you constantly give a teen input that he's a great kid, attractive, and trustworthy, he will internalize that and adopt those qualities, and the confidence that comes with them. If you choose to find fault and recite those faults to the kid day in and day out, how do you think your teen will respond?

It's like programming a computer. If you input good data, you get good results. If you input bad data, you get bad results. If you tell a teen that she'll never amount to anything, eventually she'll figure that is her destiny. Unless there is some powerful intervention from an adult who is more caring and responsible than you, that teen may never recover her sense of responsibility and self-worth.

My seventh grade math teacher, Mr. Piedmont, believed that if he showed that he expected us to perform at the highest levels, we would respond by working our butts off to meet his standards and learn more math in the process. Well, a few weeks into the school year, everyone in our class came to the realization that Mr. Piedmont had set the bar way too high. We reached for it, but time after time we fell flat on our fractions.

Mr. Piedmont got frustrated. He told us we couldn't find the hypotenuse of a triangle with both hands and an abacus. He said we were mathematical mutts. What a great strategy that was.

The class's morale took a dive as we realized that As and Bs were simply out of reach. It didn't take us long to figure out that we were never going to please Mr. Piedmont, so we quit trying. It became a joke. We were the C-Team and proud of it.

In the face of impossibly high standards, we lowered ours. My standard for homework became "Why work all night for a high C when I can watch *The Simpsons*, play with the dog, turn in early, and still get a low C?

When you find fault, you poison a relationship and risk losing your teen's respect altogether. Here are a few behaviors that describe "faultfinders." Do you see yourself in any of these characteristics?

Faultfinders:

- Take pleasure in pointing out the faults of their teen.
- Justify their poisonous ways: "I hate being so negative, but it's for their own good."
- Insist on the last word in defining what is right and wrong.
- Pick sides by recruiting other parents, friends, or whoever will support their faultfinding strategies.
- Have difficulty saying positive things to their teens.

Faultfinding is a sick and nasty game. It may make the parent feel superior to or in control of the beaten-down teen, but the long-term results can be disastrous. In truth, if you are compelled to consistently find fault with your teen, you are obviously trying to mask your own insecurities and lack of control. Sadly, most teens aren't sophisticated enough to see through your bull. They trust you. They look up to you. So they believe what you say.

But one day, this poisonous behavior will cause your teen to strike back at you. Don't be surprised when that happens. Don't wonder what went wrong. You went wrong. You poisoned your own relationship. You destroyed an opportunity to build confidence and self-respect into your teen. I hope you can live with that.

Parent Poison No. 3:

Denying responsibility for influencing your teen

Even the biggest hell-raiser of a teen wasn't born cynical or combative. That "Life Sucks" tattoo isn't a birthmark, it's the mark of a teen rebelling against his parents. Defiance is a learned behavior.

You control your child's environment from birth. You teach your child how to react and respond to life's stimuli. You install the buttons, and you push them.

"What happened to my teenager?"

You did.

A teen's character is determined by many and varied influences. But you, the parent, are number one. If the kid's a sociopath, you, Dr. Frankenstein, are the creator of that sociopath. Maybe you were there every day. Maybe you were a part-time, long-distance, see-you-on-the-Fourth-of-July kind of parent. Whatever. The kid is your doing.

Don't blame him until you take responsibility for your own mistakes. If it's not too late, you have to step up, acknowledge that you screwed up, and start taking this responsibility seriously.

Your teen is a unique individual being raised in a complex world. You can't control everything. You can't understand everything. But you know your child better than anyone else. I'm not saying that every one of your teen's flaws is your fault, or that you purposely screwed him up. I'm saying that it does no good to blame the kid. His best chance is to have you on his side, working with him, not against him. Nurturing him, not poisoning him.

I tell you this because now you can decide to do something different to get the results that you truly want. As Maya Angelou says, "When you know better, you do better." I want you to know better so that as your teen matures, you can contribute to his or her development.

Decide right now that you will no longer ignore your role in shaping who your teen is and what sort of person your teen becomes. Be a positive force in your teen's life. Recognize your power to help your child be the person you want him or her to be.

As teens, we are looking for guidance and answers. There is no place we would rather find it than in our own parents. Your teens *will* look to you, and you *will* influence them for the rest of your life. The only question is whether you will nurture them or corrupt them.

Parent Poison No. 4:

Smoke and mirrors

In a previous chapter, I noted that arguments and disagreements between parents and teens are not necessarily bad things when done in a controlled, nonhurtful way. They clear the air. They express feelings and concerns. They allow you both to vent.

But there is one particularly poisonous topic that never leads to a positive outcome: an argument over nothing.

Sometimes parents and teens become frustrated and fearful when dealing with serious issues. You see it on TV movies of the week all the time. A father has been fired from his job. He doesn't know how to tell his family. So he goes home and blows up at little Billy because he drew a picture of Barney on the wall.

Parents pick on teens over little things because they're safe. You argue over general topics because specific issues are too explosive to touch. I met a mother and daughter recently who said they fight every day "about something." No, I thought, you are fighting about nothing.

They said their disputes are usually about mother Susan's dissatisfaction with daughter Lori's grades or her "attitude" or her choice of friends. This parent-teen pair said they'd been having at least one knock-

79

down, drag-out fight every day for the last six months. Lori told me that she felt helpless because no matter what she did, no matter what changes she made to appease her mom, there was still something to fight about.

After talking to Susan for just a short period, it became very clear that she couldn't care less about all of the things she and Lori had argued about. Her fear of losing control of her increasingly self-reliant grown-up little girl was the real issue. But she was afraid to face her insecurity and fears about the approaching end of her daily parental routine. She was afraid that if she talked to her daughter about it, her fears would become more "real."

People find so many ways to mess up a relationship, even when they're trying to hang on to it. Susan loved her daughter so much, she didn't want to lose her to adulthood. But she hid her love and concern and instead poisoned their relationship by picking at her for no good reason. I convinced Susan that she had an easy choice to make: she could send her daughter off with her support and love, or she could watch her run away from a nagging, nasty, hurtful mother.

As it turned out, Lori had feared that her mother was trying to drive her away. She was confused and angry about their poisoned relationship, which had been strong through most of her teen years. Luckily they finally dispensed with the smoke and mirrors and opened up to each other. Lori will grow up, and she will become independent, but at least now she can do so with the love and support of her mother.

80

When you hide your true feelings behind smoke and mirrors, you poison your relationship. You never get to the real problem or the real solution. You give your teen every reason to strike back or to run from you. Go ahead and argue about the things that matter. Be passionate when appropriate, when something is worth fighting for.

Parent Poison No. 5:

Giving up

The ink on my driver's license has been dry for only a few years now, so I think I can speak for teenagers when I say that "Hey, we're not perfect."

We can be stubborn and belligerent. We tend to treat freshly acquired knowledge as if it were wisdom handed down only to us. We tend to patronize our parents as dolts and ancients lost in time.

But we're scared to death that you might give up on us, chuck the whole parent thing and drive off into the sunset without leaving us the keys to the house.

We can sense when you're thinking that. Sometimes we can't help but push you closer to the door. We're testing you. But we want you to pass. We don't want you to take the bait and bolt. It's just that we keep testing to see if we have any control. It's scary not being in control. So to get your attention, we ignore you. To bring you closer, we push you away. To show our love, we give you our defiance.

So why are you so confused?

Teens act out the old adage: get to them before they get to you. It comes out of our inner conflicts over the changes we're going through. One day, we want to play dolls, the next we're shopping for lipstick and eye shadow. We know that we're hard to like at this stage, so we try to give you good reason to run. We're scared that you'll give up on us first, so we act as if we don't care. It doesn't make sense. That's why the adolescent years are called the "terrible teens." Be patient. Stick with us. And don't poison the relationship by falling for our little act.

You may be in danger of doing that if you say these things to your teen:

- I'm sick of your attitude.
- I've had it with you.
- I don't know how much more of this I can take.
- You're lucky that I still put up with you.
- I can't take this anymore.

81

Them's fighting words, Ma and Pa. They show that we're getting to you with our crazed and confused teen ways. The worst thing you could ever do is to tell us by words or deeds that you have given up on us. Our mentality says that we have to win this tug-of-war at any cost. If we think for a second that we are going to lose you, we will do everything possible to drive you away. Scare us, and we will burn you down. Love us, stick with us, and the rewards will come.

6

TEENAGE LAND MINES

$\mathbf{T}$eenagers are like perennial political candidates. It seems as if we're always stumping for the parent vote. We are constantly trying to win parents over by demonstrating that we're mature, responsible, and deserving of another term. The last thing we want to do is make a mistake that betrays our general ineptitude. We're afraid that if we take one false step we'll get sent back to the seventh-grade student council.

The adult world really should issue teens Life Learner's Permits and cut us more slack. I've had friends, especially girlfriends, who've gone postal about parental scrutiny. They became obsessive about not making mistakes because they don't want to give any ammo to their parents. They put so much pressure on themselves that a raised eyebrow from Dad sends them screaming into six months of therapy.

But I don't blame them much. Teens can't afford to slip up. About the age of 14, you realize that your mistakes are magnified in your parents' eyes. Those parents who are paying attention—and they are not exactly a majority these days—do everything but perch on rooftops and track us by satellite. It's as though they're certain that any moment we'll be lured into some dangerous cult (other than the audiovisual or chess clubs) or that we'll take up an evil habit like washing our hair only every other day or going commando during tennis lessons.

It's nice to have parents who are tuned in, but when they are on full teen alert, it can be maddening. The slightest slipup brings down the wrath of Parent Person, the portly avenger. If we miss curfew, spill a lava lamp on the carpet, or lose a homework assignment out Mr. Gates's Windows, it's curtains. We're talking major consequences here. No "quiet times" for us. Younger shorties don't pay like we do. Wreck your bike, clip off all the neighbor's roses, use Dad's Big Bertha to mix paint, the little kids pay in peanuts. No *Sesame Street* for two days? Peanuts, I'm telling you!

Teens do hard time. Tough love, baby. Once you hit the adult shoe sizes, they expect you to take it like a man. Now it gets serious. The folks are panicked because it's dawned on them: You're just a couple years from college. They're going to have to fork up thousands and thousands of dollars for your higher education, and if they don't get your butt under control, you might blow off classes and shoot pool in a biker bar all day!

Because our parents are so hyperworried, interacting with them is like dirty dancing through a minefield. You'd better know where those land mines are, my friends. You do what you have to do to get where you want to go. So, in this chapter specially formatted to fit your book page, we are going to identify the land mines that can cause you to self-destruct right before your parents' eyes. Watch your step as we leave the staging area, and remember, don't stick your arms out too far, they might go home in another car.

Teen Land Mine No. 1:

Thinking you're a lost cause

One of the major ways that we blow the tenuous teen-parent connection is by letting self-destructive thoughts sabotage our relationship. Let me list a few of these land mines for you.

- I'm never going to please them.
- They hate me.

TEENAGE LAND MINES

- **We're never going to get along.**
- **My family life sucks.**

Not exactly uplifting inner dialogue, is it? That sort of negative thinking is sure to drag you down, and if your parents are paying any attention at all, they'll pick up on it. When you convince yourself that your parents are so mean or so uncool that you could never get along with them, you are doing the land-mine rumba. With that attitude, things are going to blow in no time. Get out the white chalk and the yellow police tape. Call the coroner. Your relationship with your parents is DOA.

My high school basketball coach always told us that if we started a game thinking there was no way we could win, then we'd already lost. It works the same way with the Parent Trap. If you decide that you're miserable doing time with Mom and Dad, then there's not a chance in Hell that you're going to find happy times at home.

Don't change your attitude for your parents' sake, my sake, or the sake of the great state of West Virginia. Do it because it makes sense for you. Do it because hanging your head down is bad for your posture. Do it because it makes life better for you.

A friend told me that getting along with his parents was like knowing the names of the Teletubbies. You should never admit to it! To be seen hanging with your folks at the mall was to be forever consigned to outer Dorkville, according to this parent-averse guy. Of course, he didn't seem to mind driving around in his dad's car, using his dad's credit card, or wearing the clothes his mother washed and ironed for him. I'd say he was confused about a few things, wouldn't you? Or else he was just being a jerk to his parents.

Dork or jerk? Not much of a choice, is it?

It may be uncool to dress like your parents, to listen to the music they like, or to otherwise adopt their premillennial mannerisms, but it is not uncool to get along with the people who provided your DNA, not to mention last night's dinner. Give your relationship with these strange but lovable people a chance. Think long term. If you alienate them now, who's going to walk you down the aisle at your wedding, the FedEx guy? Who's going to take your kids fishing and spoil them rotten with candy? Remember, it's never a bad deal to get along with the people who make the decisions about your freedom—and who may one day pass on their vast estate, including the cherry-colored Plymouth Valiant in the garage.

Decide that your relationship with your parents *will* work and that you *will* be happy with them. Keep in mind that just because you're unhappy does not necessarily mean that your parents are the cause of your unhappiness. You have to take responsibility for your attitude and your approach to life. Blaming them hasn't gotten you anywhere special so far, has it? So get off it and get going.

Teen Land Mine No. 2:

Thinking you're smarter than your parents

The following is an actual teen parent–to–teen parent conversation recorded by our hidden microphone under a poolside table somewhere in the midwestern United States:

Teen Parent A: So your boy's sixteen now?

Teen Parent B: Yeah, and I'm getting more stupid by the day.

The truth hurts, doesn't it? Especially when you're a parent.

In a national survey conducted at my high school lunch table (yes, *that* lunch table), it was determined that today's teenagers actually are—with only a few minor exceptions involving inbreeding by royalty—150 percent smarter than the average parent! The evidence is simply overwhelming:

- They grew up with only three networks on television. We have cable.
- They had battery-operated walkie-talkies. We have the Internet.

- They had never even seen a **VCR**. We have the entire Nintendo and PlayStation universes.
- They had big black rotary phones. We have pagers, blackberries, and cell phones galore.

I rest my case. We are Mister Spocks to our parents' Captain Kirks. We are more highly developed life-forms because our universe is bigger than their universe. We've had far more opportunities and more challenges. Witness our favorite television show, *Jackass*. The parent mind simply can't grasp the complexities and intellectual depth of young men jumping into shopping carts and rolling down hills. It's a shame that so many adults are missing out, but it is simply beyond them.

There is, however, some trace evidence that our parents actually do have brains with the capacity to expand. My father, for one, is adamant that his personal model is "in fact bigger than the brain of a field mouse." I have to step in here and back him up on this. He was smart enough to turn his teenage book franchise over to me after I spent many long hours persuading him that he is, in fact, too old to write books for teenagers. Still, my dad does have a knack for coming up with insights into and innovative approaches to human foibles. He has a certain depth of experience that seems to compensate for his lack of training on PlayStation. Every now and then he comes up with something approaching wisdom. He's particularly proud of this one: "The more you know, the more you realize what you didn't know before."

That's parent patois for "When you get to be my age, you're realize what an azz you were at 16." One of the things I've realized in dealing with parental life-forms, outdated as they may be, is that they tend to bristle at being treated as our intellectual inferiors. They make the case that their broader and deeper range of experience keeps them in the game. I've spent hours racking my brain to come up with some examples to support their contention, and I did identify one within my own immediate family.

In the summer before my first year of high school football, my dad

87

told me that I needed to run so I'd be in shape by the time practice started in the fall. I thought this was perhaps the dumbest idea I'd heard since New Coke. So I ignored his suggestion and limited my physical activity to sunbathing and the occasional walk to the snack counter to tone my calves.

As you might expect, I sucked wind for the first six weeks of football practice, though I did get nice comments on my tan and the robust condition of my calves. So, based on that smidgen of evidence, one might draw the rather broad inference that within a certain frame of reference, our parents may have a worthwhile thought or two. I'm not sure that conclusion is based on solid science, but we'll go with the circumstantial evidence here.

Parents do have a much different perspective. Sometimes when we think they are flat-out wrong, it is really more a matter of their different experiences. My dad had played high school football already. I hadn't. He knew that if I didn't get into shape, I was going to be heaving into my helmet after the first set of wind sprints. He was right.

So there you have it. It pains me to say that we may need to consider our parents' opinions now and then, or at least feign interest in what they have to say. I recommend this for a couple of reasons.

First, if we consider what our parents have to say, they're much more likely to consider what we have to say. I don't know about you, but I grew to appreciate that my dad didn't go deaf when I asked for a curfew extension.

Second, if we always come at them from the position that they don't know squat, our parents may pick up on that and respond in a manner that could have a long-term and detrimental impact on our continuing ability to breath through our noses.

Sure, our world is very different from what our parents' world was when they were our age, but that's not their fault. Let me throw out a wild card here: What if, as we grow older, some of the things our parents have said and done start to make sense—in retrospect? Stranger things have happened, you know. Shakespeare's teenagers thought his plays were positively Elizabethan. Picasso's kids told him his paintings were square.

For the sake of family unity, if nothing else, give your parents credit for having at least the mental capacity of a field mouse. It makes my dad feel better. And when Dad feels good about himself, we, as a nation, sleep a lot easier.

Teen Land Mine No. 3:

Unleashing anger at your parents

My buddy Mark gets so mad at his parents whenever they discipline him that it's embarrassing to be around him. Once he went to a party when he was grounded. There was nothing "bad" going on at the party, but he wasn't supposed to leave the house, so he was in technical violation of his punishment according to Robert's Rules of Grounding.

When his folks drove up, I heard this eerie, twinkling music playing in my head. Then I looked at Mark. He actually became the little girl in the bed from *The Exorcist*. He raged. He spewed. I swear his head did a 360 while the rest of his body remained perfectly still. He called his parents names that hurt *my* feelings.

It was definitely the highlight of an otherwise dull party. Mark and his parents argued out on the lawn for nearly an hour before his dad got him into the car and took him home. I figured we'd hear later that they'd signed him up for the French Foreign Legion or the next NASA flight to Mars.

Mark called a few days after the confrontation. He said he was not going to speak to his parents until he was allowed out of the house—which should be around his thirty-fifth birthday, according to a poll taken at the party.

Mark was obviously wrong, even according to a jury of his peers. He should not have gone to that party while grounded. But I think his dumbest move was throwing that Stage V tantrum at his parents. He made a bad situation a lot worse. He embarrassed himself in front of his friends and more than a few strangers. (I hope he never meets one of them at a job interview.)

Mark isn't the smartest monkey at the zoo (sorry, Mark), but I think the dumbest thing I have ever seen him do is call his mom some really vile names that night. It was as if he wanted to make sure his parents stayed mad at him for the next six years. What he just doesn't understand is that when you do things that are really outrageously disrespectful—such as calling your mom a name borrowed from the canine vernacular—your parents won't forget. Had he just gone home and calmly talked to his parents, he might have fared a whole lot better.

Your parents will probably get over it if you come home late or bring home a C in math, but they won't *ever* forget being screamed and cursed at by their own kid. When you lose it and unload on your parents, the overwhelming odds are that you are only going to:

1. Dig yourself a much deeper hole.
2. Look like a spoiled brat in need of a kick in the ass.

Anger was allegedly a good idea in the early days of the human race. It fired you up with adrenaline so you could fight or flee, depending on the size of the prehistoric thing wanting to eat you. But I'm not so sure that these days anyone under 21 should be allowed to operate under the influence of anger. It just seems to get us into more trouble.

Parents do not respond well to it at all. You yell at them, they yell back. You slam a door, they slam your weekend plans. Which reminds me, the first time this girl I know slammed her bedroom door in anger, her father calmly opened it and said, "If you do that again, I will remove this door from its hinges." A week or two later, she lost her temper again. Ran to her room and slammed the door. Up came her dad with a screwdriver and tap hammer. Off came the door. For three weeks, she had to live an exposed life. Even when her friends came over, there was no door to hide behind. Once it went back up, she never slammed it again.

Don't step on a land mine by unleashing anger and hostility at your parents. It does no good. It only puts you deeper in the hole. They really don't want to punish you, particularly if you demonstrate regret and apologize. But it's much easier for them to punish your anger. They undoubtedly love you, but they hate your anger. They don't mind that your anger doesn't get to go to Homecoming, but they would like to see you there.

It's an even bigger mistake to hold a grudge and stay mad at your parents. It only reminds them that you broke the rules. It doesn't buy you an early release. It sure doesn't have any great impact on *their* lives. And holding a grudge is just plain hard work. It makes your jaws sore. Look in the mirror. The grudge face is not at all attractive, is it? So get over it. Admit you screwed up. Take your punishment like a grown-up. If you don't want to do the time, don't do the crime. And don't sabotage yourself by holding on to your anger.

Teen Land Mine No. 4:

Playing mind games

Nikki made a deal with her dad on her sixteenth birthday: he agreed to buy her a car if she would pay the insurance premiums. Seemed like a good deal to me. Her dad got her exactly the car she wanted, and her premium payments, because they were on his policy, were only a couple hundred dollars a year (insurance companies stick it to teens, by the way).

But from the beginning, Nikki plotted to make it an even better deal. She never intended to pay the insurance. She knew that if she didn't pay the bills, her father would. So she threw them away. She figured she'd get grounded, and she did, but she never paid a dime for the insurance on her car.

Nikki bragged to me that she'd pulled one off on her parents. I made a mental note never to get involved in a business deal with Nikki. I'd say she'd have no trouble becoming a board-certified brat. Maybe she manipulated her father, maybe he just let it happen. Either way, I'm sure he learned that she was not trustworthy or appreciative.

If she lost her father's trust and respect just to get a new car and duck the insurance payments, I don't think she made much of a deal at

91

all. What she did was very shortsighted, among other things. I'm sure her father didn't ask her to pay the insurance premiums because he couldn't afford to do it. He wanted her to take some responsibility. She blew it off.

My philosophy is that you can earn more than you could ever steal. If Nikki had accepted the responsibility her father gave her, he probably would have been more willing to help her out in the future. As it is, I think he'd be a fool to give her anything else.

Nikki was exhibiting passive-aggressive behavior in playing games with her father's trust and generosity. Playing games like that can ruin your relationships. Passive-aggressive people often make promises with no intention of keeping them. They aggressively go after what they want, and then, when they get it, they back away from any responsibility for maintaining it. This includes friendships, partnerships, and business deals.

Here are a few characteristics of passive-aggressive game-playing teens. Do you see any of these characteristics in yourself?

- Are you always trying to get more out of your parents?
- Do you enjoy manipulating your parents to get your way?
- Do you consider yourself craftier or smarter than your parents?
- If you are asked to do something you don't want to do, do you pretend to be no good at it?

Teens who play games often get what they want for a while, but they usually end up driving people away and sabotaging their relationships. Parents wise up quickly too. They may stick with you because they love you without qualification. But that doesn't mean they will trust or respect you if you abuse their love.

Manipulating others may be fun to you, but it is no fun to them. Trust is hard to come by. Purposely betraying a trust is both ruthless and gutless. It's a land mine.

Teen Land Mine No. 5:

Being a high-maintenance teen

Sandy's mother found her sitting on her bed in a sweatshirt, staring out the window. "What's wrong, honey? We're ready to go to your little brother's first soccer game. Aren't you coming?"

"Mom, do you know that Matt is refusing to wear that really cute soccer shirt I gave him for his birthday?"

"But Sandy, they have uniforms. They can't play unless they wear them."

"Well, he could at least wear it under his team jersey, couldn't he?"

The issue here is not little Matt's choice of clothing. It is Sandy's need to be the focus of each and every family outing. Sandy is insecure. She is needy. She is higher maintenance than the typical aircraft carrier.

She sucks the life out of her relationship with her parents and everyone else who gets close to her. Insecurity is a repulsive characteristic. Needy people are chronically self-centered. Every family conversation, every trip, every event, everything that happens anywhere is always about them and their needs.

Here are some expressions common to the high-maintenance teen:

93

- What about *my* feelings?
- I'm not ready yet.
- Open my present first.
- You made me feel bad.
- Dad would do anything for *you.*
- It's not my fault we're late.
- I don't want to go with them, they make me nervous.
- What do you think I should do?
- Do you think I'm ever going to get it right?
- Why can't you go with me right now?

- We quit seeing each other. He was never there for me.
- You didn't say a thing about how nice I look.
- You told him he played a good game, but you didn't mention my home run.

Then there is the classic high-maintenance line: "Well, enough about me . . . what do *you* think of me?"

Being high maintenance is almost as bad as being radioactive. Once people figure out that you are infected with insecurity and neediness, they'll put on metal chest protectors to ward off your bad vibes. High-maintenance people often make it impossible for others to relax and enjoy themselves because they demand to be the center of attention at all times.

If you notice people wandering off while you are talking about yourself, take it as a sign that you've entered the high-maintenance mine field. If you make such unreasonable demands on your friends that they can't possibly please you, take a refresher course in personal diplomacy.

Parents of high-maintenance teens have been known to spend the summers in France—or even south Texas—just to get away. Chronic insecurity prevents some teens from leaving the nest, or even leaving the bedroom. And it isn't that they truly believe they are unworthy. That's just a tool they use to get attention. They crave attention. If they aren't at the center, they crumble like dried-up Silly Putty.

High-maintenance people never reciprocate all the attention they demand. They don't fulfill their part of a relationship. They are relentless takers. Stingy givers. No one can ever support them enough or appreciate them enough. Anything that is not a compliment is an insult. They want more, more, more.

They'll sell their souls to feed their egos. High-maintenance teens don't play fair. They claim the status of a young adult but demand that their parents give them the same attention they had as children. They lean on their parents so much it drags them down. They sabotage their relationship with their parents by refusing to grow up and take responsibility for their own happiness.

Here are some characteristics of high-maintenance teens:

- They allow any form of criticism to knock them totally off track.
- They sense rejection everywhere.
- They claim to be incompetent even at things they're good at.
- They don't get angry; they get hurt and very dramatic.
- They pretend not to have a preference but manipulate others to get what they want.

If you catch yourself in these behaviors, I suggest you do a little soul-searching. If not, you are going to make a tough life for yourself. High-maintenance people have such impossible standards for happiness that they are almost never content with their lives or their relationships. People become exhausted dealing with their fragile psyches and their constant craving for assurance and praise. It's almost impossible to have a meaningful conversation with someone who can take any innocent comment as a devastating criticism.

So take down the high-maintenance sign. Give other people the opportunity to breathe naturally in your presence. Stop the childish games and grow up. I promise you will live happily ever after. But what about me? Do I seem okay to you? Hey wait, where are you going? I'm not done talking about me yet! Wait! I'll go with you . . .

7

PARENT DOS AND DON'TS

Heads up!

It's been brought to our attention here at Parent-Teen Relationship Rescue that some of you parents and teens are in need of a little refresher course. It seems that you have managed to forget a few of the basics regarding what you should be doing and—*au contraire*—what you should not be doing regarding your behavior toward each other.

To refresh your memories and keep you on track, I have put together some quick and easy points. This chapter deals with the Dos and Don'ts for parents. Chapter 8 does the same for you teens. Many of the points covered here are simply reinforcements of the major points I've harped about so far in this book. Due to the limitations of the print medium, I can't beat them into you, so endless repetition is the next best thing. You might want to staple these to your favorite household pet or stencil them onto your car as a way to always keep them fresh in your mind.

It would benefit both the parent reader and the teen reader to study these two chapters just to see what you should expect from each other in the way of considerate treatment. Please read all the entries. Commit them to memory. Have them crocheted into your goatee if that will help. There will be a test later, but it won't be coming from me. You will be testing each other, as usual.

Of course, this is all part of our full-service package, for which you will be charged extra when we figure out exactly how to do that without taking hostages.

The Dos List

1. Have a clear boundary between your parent role and your buddy role.

To paraphrase the ancient and purple philosopher, Barney the Dinosaur:

I love you.

You love me.

But I'm not your buhuhu-dee.

You can be a friend to your child. But unless you are Eddie Murphy, you can't play both roles at the same time, all the time. Sooner or later, parent and buddy are going to clash. Each role has its purpose. Each is a caring presence. But a teen should be able to tell his buddy anything without being judged. Parents are incapable of withholding judgment when it comes to their teens. They have too much invested emotionally.

Buddies are people you sometimes go to just to vent your innermost feelings. You need protection from prosecution when you do that. It's like lawyer-client or priest-confessor confidentiality. Parents and teens don't match up well in that sort of relationship. Be a good friend to your child. But keep in mind that a teen can find buddies in many places. Good parents are extremely rare.

2. Be involved.

"But I am involved!" Oh yeah? You asked for it.

Pop quiz!!!

- **Who is your teen's homeroom teacher?**
- **What's the name of the last CD your teen purchased?**

- Who is the artist?
- Was it the radio version or the uncensored version of the CD?
- What's your teen's favorite subject in school?
- Who is her/his favorite teacher?
- Who does your teen eat lunch with every day at school? (This is a big deal in the social hierarchy, you know.)
- What are your teen's favorite Web sites?

If you answered every one of those questions correctly and without polling the audience or phoning a friend, then you honestly are truly involved in your child's life. Don't let it go to your head. Being involved with your teen means being there even when it isn't easy, even when it's not convenient, and even when they aren't particularly interested in having you around. Mostly, it's about knowing what is going on in your teen's life and in her heart and mind. And it's about keeping the lines of communication open at all times so that if something really important comes up, your teen will come to you without fear or apprehension.

3. Make your teen accountable.

It is your responsibility to prepare your teens for life after an allowance and the carefree joys of free room and board. You don't want them graduating from college and then calling you with postgraduate syndrome. That's when they suffer flashbacks to the life of a kept kid. They begin craving whatever is in your refrigerator and, worse, their old bedroom. You don't want to hear the four scariest words a 21-year-old can utter to a parent: "I'm moving back home!"

To keep that from happening and screwing up your golden years, you have to do a little groundwork. It involves teaching your teens that if they want to live a certain lifestyle, they have to attain a certain level of performance. This is not so much about money as it is about responsibility, independence, and self-sufficiency.

Set up a system in which your teen earns an allowance, bonus points, or whatever carrot you want to dangle by performing useful tasks around the house. Don't mess with their minds. If they do the job correctly, give them the agreed-upon reward. Help them form a view of the world as it exists outside the benevolence of the home. Get them to understand that when they perform consistently they can predict what their rewards will be.

Let them see that when they choose certain behaviors, they choose the consequences that go with them. When they work, they get paid. When they don't do the job, they don't get the reward. That is teaching them how the world works.

4. Listen to and hear your teen's point of view.

The key is to listen with the goal of understanding. Just hearing what was said doesn't count. I hear hundreds of sounds as I walk down the street, but do I take the time to understand what each one of them means? Surveys of teens' attitudes toward their parents always include laments that their parents rarely give them their full attention and even when they do listen to them, they do it in a judgmental way. They respond with their own opinions rather than making an effort to "get it" from the teens' perspective.

This is important stuff. You need to get it right because if you don't listen when your teen tries to communicate, he'll go somewhere else. You don't want that. The next time your teen plops down next to your desk or your reading chair, stop what you are doing and focus on not only the words being spoken but also the emotions and implications behind them. Listen so well that you could repeat everything back nearly word for word if you had to. Don't interrupt. If your teen's words are argumentative, rebellious, irreverent, or disrespectful—as if *that* won't happen—try to focus on the goal here. Give your teen some slack, hear him or her, and then home in on the message that lies beneath the heated rhetoric. Very often, that message is a cry for help. Keep this in mind: You are the grown-up here.

5. Tell them your logic and reasoning for making decisions.

You don't owe your teen an explanation of why you've made a decision regarding his or her activities. You do owe yourself the opportunity to give that explanation to your teen. Look, the kid needs to know the process for making informed and good decisions in his own life. If you simply lay down the law and say, "Do it because I told you to!," what have you given that teen? Nothing more than a command. That's fine if you're a Navy SEAL lieutenant and your teen commandos are on a mission in enemy territory. In that case, all they need to know is their assigned duties. But as a parent you are preparing to send a young person out into the world, and it is *your* duty to give her a basis for making her own thoughtful decisions.

So the next time you're tempted to practice the command-and-control method with your teen, think again about what your long-term responsibility as a parent is. Think about the real gift you give a teen when you explain that you are demanding his return home at midnight because the hours between midnight and 3 A.M. are the most deadly for teen drivers. It's not because you don't trust him but because at that hour the streets and highways are teeming with maniac drivers, carjackers, and jumpy patrolmen. You want your teen off the street because you want him safe and sound. There aren't many teens who won't accept that reasoning, and even those who don't accept it as teens will respect it as adults.

6. Stand up for your teen.

Don't leave your kid dangling. There are times when you need to step up and be the heavy and tell his friend he's not going. Don't leave it to the kid to take the brunt. My dad told a story that makes this point clear. He grew up in Kansas, and there was a basketball game in Lawrence, about thirty miles away. There was a huge ice storm moving in. He and his friend John were heading out of the house to the game, which they figured to be about an hour and half away. My granddad said whoa: "Where ya'll going?"

The boys explained that the big game was going to be played that night, so they were leaving early. He said, "You aren't going anywhere. The roads are already icy and the sun just went down. There's no way you're going out on that highway just for a game."

After the obligatory arguing they went back up to the bedroom.

101

Dad was a little embarrassed at being yanked off the road by his father in front of his friend. But John, who was a very rough-and-tumble guy, didn't give him any flak about it. In fact, he got real quiet. Dad saw that he was staring out the bedroom window and his eyes were teared up.

Dad actually thought John was so mad he was going to cry, but that wasn't what was going on. Dad told John he could go ahead to the game without him, but John said, "You don't know what it would mean to me if my parents cared enough to tell me I couldn't go out on a night like this. I could tell them I was going to drive to the North Pole, and they wouldn't look up from the newspaper."

Everybody needs a champion, and that champion should be the parent. Your teen needs to know you are in his or her corner. Stand up for your teens when they need it. They won't forget.

7. Stay tuned to your teen's world.

Have you heard some of the lyrics of the most popular rap songs? Did you know that many are banned from radio? Some come with two sets of lyrics, one for radio play, the other for private play. Do you know which version your teen is listening to? That's part of your responsibility.

Tune in, not only to their musical tastes and purchases but to everything they're involved in. You should know the names of their friends—and the names of their parents. When was the last time you walked through your teen's bedroom and checked it out? Have you ever checked their e-mail files? Their downloaded files? If you haven't, then you aren't fulfilling your responsibilities.

Before I spent the night somewhere, my parents always talked to the people involved. If my mother called and some dip answered the phone, she would veto the sleepover. "They can come here if you want to spend the night together," she'd say.

8. Show flexibility.

It's good to have rules, but sometimes the situation outgrows the rule. These times call for flexibility. If your teen is forbidden to drive after midnight, what happens when he's kept late at work and can't get home unless he breaks the rule? Flexibility demonstrates your wisdom.

9. Find common interests.

I used to watch reruns of the old *Andy Griffith Show,* which always had an introductory scene that showed Andy fishing with his son, Opie. I was always envious of that boy. My dad didn't fish. We didn't even eat fish unless it came in the form of a fish stick. For the longest time, I thought fish came in sticks. My first trip to the aquarium was a revelation!

Now I understand what appealed to me about that *Andy Griffith Show* opening. It wasn't the whistled theme song, it was the camaraderie of father and son. Opie and Andy.

There are two reasons for developing some interest with your teen, whether it's fishing, golf, or renovating an old sports car. First of all, shared interests lead to new levels of understanding. They introduce a new vocabulary that you can share. Second, the shared interests put you on a more level playing field as you learn together and share experiences. I am not talking about becoming bosom buddies and checking out the babes at Hooters together. You might want to find something a little more positive than that.

A girlfriend of mine got her dad interested in making jewelry, and they worked together to turn out some great stuff. She got a double benefit because she could wear the rings and necklaces as well as create some things for her friends. I also know a mother who helped her son start a band. Believe it or not, your teen wants to have some connection with you besides arguing over the car keys. Take the responsibility to find something to share.

10. Deliver your messages even when your teen won't listen.

This is one of those secrets teens have that I am very hesitant to divulge for fear that my teen buddies will consider me as a traitor, but believe it or not, teens do listen to their parents. Even when we howl and scream that you don't know what you're talking about, even when we slam the door behind us, your words stick.

Even when we hold our hands to our ears, your words will be remembered. That does not mean that we will submit to all of your pronouncements and opinions, nor does it mean that we will believe everything you tell us. But the law of teen neurology demands that we remember. I remember stuff that my parents have told from the time I was born that still doesn't make any sense, but I remember it. Maybe one of these days I'll figure it out and then I can decide what to do with it, but for now, it stays with or without my consent.

Your job is to say what you have to say, regardless of who is listening. Tell me your values on smoking, doping, sex, and everything else I need to learn from you, and it will get through. It may not look that way because teens do not exactly have the precise behavior of scholars, you know. And if you don't, you have neglected me.

The Don'ts List

These are the reminders of the traps that you can get into if you don't read the signs. I'm fresh out of the teenagers' world. I can still view things from their perspective, I know that as a parent, if you don't walk and talk smart, you may be walking and talking to someone else.

1. Don't take a hands-off approach.

I don't care what it takes, you have no right to throw up your hands and abandon your parental responsibilities. Your teen may spit in your eye, slam the door so hard the house falls down, and drive your car into the Rio Grande; you are still a parent and you have to do your duty.

There are two things in your favor: One, eventually the kid is going to grow up . . . and it is said that anyone who raises a teen gets a free ticket to Heaven because they have already gone through Hell. Two, one day your teen will realize that either you've gotten smarter with old age or you weren't ever as stupid as he thought you were.

These are small consolations, but you have to take what you can get.

2. Don't tell your teens what they want to hear.

Teens aren't rational a lot of the time because their hormones are running amok and their brains are rewiring themselves. They know they're out of control and borderline nuts. So they're betting on you to save them from themselves. They need an adult's perspective and judgment. They don't want to be allowed to self-destruct. It's your job to tell them what they don't want to hear because it is what they really want to hear.

They may get mad, but they will get over it. Remember that parenting is not a popularity contest. You are not doing this to get votes for Parent of the Year. Don't give your teen what she wants, give her what she needs.

3. Don't be a buddy, be a parent.

You can be a friend to your child without being a buddy. A friend protects you and tells you when you are going down the wrong road. A buddy goes along for the ride. A friend says, "You can't do that!" A buddy says, "What time do you want to get going?"

If you try to be a buddy to your child, you will only confuse him. Be a friend and a protector, but play the parent all the way. Let your teens know that your job isn't to make them happy, it is to keep them safe.

4. Don't expect teens to deal with adult decisions.

Parents often expect adult behavior from teens who have grown to the size of adults. But just because they can wear the shoes doesn't mean they can handle the pressure. Your stunning 15-year-old daughter might feel she's ready to marry her 17-year-old boyfriend, but you know better. It is your duty to step in and stop her from making a huge mistake that will mess up her life. She wants and needs help with her decisions. Marriage is an adult decision.

5. Don't burden your children with your issues.

Your teens are not mature enough to be your sounding boards or your confidants. They can't handle it, and you should know better than to dump your adult problems and frustrations on them. That's not communication, it's abuse. Divorced parents who do this should be shot and chopped up for Doberman feed. It's bad enough that the family has come apart; don't burden your teen with adult problems.

6. Don't believe everything your teens tell you.

Think back to the little lies you told your parents when you were a teenager. What makes you think your teens aren't doing the same to you? You have to be on your guard. Don't let them take advantage. They won't respect you if they can dupe you.

7. Don't be oblivious to what temptations are available.

In high school I went to parties where they were handing out sugar cubes laced with LSD as appetizers. It was wild, and it hasn't changed. Don't be oblivious to what's going on out there. There are more temptations today than ever before. The Internet is one big porn highway, and if you aren't checking your kid's surfing habits, you're not doing your job.

8. Don't be uninvolved.

Go to your teens' schools. Go to their games. Don't be lazy as a parent. I feel strongly about this. If your teen is building a bomb in his bedroom and you don't know it, either you are an idiot or you don't care. Regardless of how much your teens protest that the Constitution covers the spaces under their beds and their closets, it's still your responsibility to know what's going on.

9. Don't let their values be set externally.

It's your job to teach your teens what is right and what is wrong. You have to make your values known. They may reject your values when they reach adulthood. That's fine, but for now you set the standards and you should expect them to live by them. Tell them what you feel about honesty, integrity, spirituality, character, and love. That's your job.

10. Don't set up a false economy.

Make your teens work for what they want. Don't just hand them one thing after another. They'll never understand it when that doesn't happen later in life. They'll think that the world owes them something, and if they take that attitude into adulthood, they'll be in for a rude awakening.

8

TEEN DOS AND DON'TS

Now it's Teen Tune-Up Time. As with the preceding chapter for parents, this is basically a refresher and warm-up course before we roll into the full-contact, helmets-and-pads part of the book.

The following lists of Dos and Don'ts provide a review of things teens can do to reconnect with their parents, and things that they should avoid doing to spoil that connection and risk being grounded unto eternity or until the Madonna Wheelchairs and Walkers Tour.

I hope you teen readers took a look at the previous chapter, which is a similar list of Dos and Don'ts for parents. If your parents aren't reading along, I'd recommend you head down to Kinko's, make a copy of that chapter, and tape it to the refrigerator or your father's golf bag.

Carefully read each of these Dos and Don'ts. Memorize them. Have them etched by a craftsman on the forehead of your closest friend for handy reference. Please prepare for takeoff by switching off all notebook computers and cell phones. Put your tray tables up. Seats in the upright position. And now, please direct your attention to the Author in the aisle as he demonstrates how to save your ass . . . I mean your relationship . . . in case of a crash and burn.

The Dos List

1. Clue your parents in when you have a decision to make.

I know, you're sweating this already. You're thinking that if you tell them what's going on, they'll just butt in. They'll try to get you to do what they want and then get mad if you don't take their advice. Well, if it's something you think they're going to blow a primary artery about, don't tell them. Of course, you're going to have to deal with them sooner or later. Pesky parents don't just go away.

So don't clue them in on your wild-ass plan to skip school and Jet-Ski to Bermuda. But do tell them if you have a less volatile decision to make, such as whether to get a job, try out for the school play, or commit a misdemeanor. You know, any of life's *little* decisions. If you're afraid they'll steamroll you, try setting some ground rules: "I want to get your input on this, but I want to make my own decisions. I'm going to be on my own before too long, and I've got to start doing that. But I'd like to hear what you think."

The point here is to try to get them involved in your life. If they haven't been there before, this might help draw them in a little. Why would you want to do that? Because whether you admit it or not, you want them there, and sooner or later you're going to need them there. I can guarantee you, they feel the same way, even if they are lousy at showing it.

Maybe things have been rotten up to now. Maybe you've given up on them. Maybe they've given up on you. What can it hurt to open the door a crack? If they can't be mature about this, show them that you can. Take the long view. No senior citizen has ever sat in a nursing home and said, "I shouldn't have tried to get closer to my parents." They aren't going to be around forever, but bitter memories can last a lifetime.

Think about this too: if you cut your parents in on the decision, they'll have to take some responsibility for it. Consider this an opportunity to show them that you have your act together. Teach them something. The key here is to open the phone lines. If you can talk about the little crap, then when the big stuff comes up you won't be left hanging all by yourself.

2. Make the first move to reconnect.

Insecurity strikes parents too. Teens aren't the only ones to feel shut out or rejected. So if you're sitting back thinking that it's up to your parents to make a connection, you're wasting valuable time. They might feel as if you don't want to have anything to do with them. After all, you've got a lot going on in your life too.

Need an opening line? "Hey Dad, did I tell you about what happened at school the other day?"

That's all it takes. If you don't get a pulse with that one, try this: "If you've got some time, I'd like to catch you up on a few things that have been going on."

Still no heartbeat? Then get sneaky: "I've got a new Internet friend. He's about to get paroled, and he needs a place to crash. What do you think?"

Sometimes life's a dopey soap opera of miscommunication, hurt feelings, and misunderstandings. Just say, "Cut!" Step up and write a new script. Be the grown-up if your parents can't handle it. It's to your advantage to initiate the connection when it works best for you. Surprise them, and they may surprise you.

111

3. Let them know you're interested in their dull, boring lives too.

The whole parents-were-once-human thing gets old. And hard to digest. Those old photographs of Dad in a wife-beater T-shirt riding a Harley with his ponytail flying in the wind are like something from another dimension. But if you're looking for ways to break the ice—and believe me, it's in your best interest—you might bait your parents with a few questions about the days before they became hard-asses.

Ask your mom about the guys she dated. Ask your dad about his athletic career. (Keep in mind that hallucinations about one's high school days are common.)

If nothing else, talking to your parents about their glory days may get you some ammunition to throw back at them later: "Well, *you* dated a guy who was a senior in college when you were a sophomore in high school, so why is it wrong for me to go out with our State Farm agent? The commercials say he's like a good neighbor!"

If you get them to talk about their lives, they might just drop their guard and start to see you as more of an equal. They may even take more of an interest in you as a human being rather than as the impending disaster sleeping down the hall.

4. Talk to your parents about the little things too.

Don't assume they'll just blow you off. When I started to get interested in taking flying lessons, I mentioned it to my dad. I figured he'd think I was just dreaming. It turned out that he was nuts about flying too. I never knew! He told me that he'd started flying when he was 11 years old—without a license, of course. He helped his father transport oil-field equipment to drill sites. I learned about how hard he worked as a kid. He flew while his father slept so they could fill orders. It helped explain his values and his determination to me.

The more you talk to each other, the stronger your bond becomes. We get frustrated when we can't express how we're feeling, and a lot of times that makes us do crazy things. If you can get that crap out of your system by talking about it, you are less likely to go postal. The shrinks call this "anger management." Fine. Call it what you like. Talking things out with your folks beats telling your story to the sentencing judge. The more you talk, the more your parents will feel connected. The more you talk, the better connection you will have.

5. Do it better. Take it further. Exceed all expectations.

Certain tactics can win you a "Get out of Jail Free" pass. Others get you thrown in The Hole. If you're hit with a midnight curfew, try getting home by 11:30. If your weekly budget is $50, come back on Saturday with a $10 surplus. If they expect you to come home with Cs on your report card, make it a clean sweep of Bs. Build up some credibility. Exceed expectations. It's like money in the bank.

Look, your relationship with your parents is one big negotiation. When you exceed expectations, you give yourself negotiating points. "I've been home a half hour early every week, would you mind if I stayed out an extra hour this Saturday so I can stay at the concert until the last song?" That's money in the bank.

Think of the limits your parents set as tests of character, not restrictions on your freedom. Don't push the envelope. Play the game. Dazzle them with your cooperation. Don't get sucked into the me-versus-you game. You can't win. They have the high ground for now. Rise up by demonstrating good faith and good intentions.

I had a friend who was an Olympic trainer. He had an international reputation for getting athletes to perform at their peak levels. He'd tell his runners to always go a little farther than required when training. He explained that if they were running the 100-yard dash and trained for 100 yards, they would want to start their finish at 90 yards, but if they trained to run 120 yards, they would still be running hard at 100.

Give it a little extra. Go for the gold. Who knows, your face may end up on a box of Wheaties!

6. Wise up.

Stop me if you've heard this one: A teenager was following his father into the forest. (Okay, so this tale is a little dated.) Just as they were entering into the thick stuff, the dad turns to the son with this advice: "If you step into some bear crap, that's life. But if you see me step into some bear crap and you still step into it too, that's stupid!"

What? You were expecting Plato? *Grimm's Fairy Tales?* It's not easy finding teen guru stories in this market, so take it easy. The point here . . . *ahem!* The *point* here is that it doesn't hurt to think of those people across the breakfast counter as potential sources of wisdom and enlightenment.

Unless there is some really weird science in your background, your

113

parents have been around longer than you, right? They've been there, done that when it comes to grade school, junior high, and high school, right?

Maybe they screwed up in the past, but if nothing else they might help spare you from making the same dumb mistakes. They may have grown up in a different era—even on a different planet—but human nature doesn't change much. They dealt with the same high school BS that you are dealing with. Bullies. Snobs. Nerds. Zits. Where to keep your eyes focused while showering in gym class . . . all the bull that's been around since Betty and Veronica were flirting with Archie and Jughead at the malt shop.

For example (no, it's not another tale from the ancient forest), the father of a friend of mine once overheard my friend tell a cute girl, "Nobody wants to go out with me." He later sat the son down and filled him in on the whole "girls like guys who are self-confident" scenario. It was a small thing, no great revelation. But it helped my friend understand the dating game a little better. It was just a matter of a father who'd learned the hard way trying to help his son have an easier time.

7. Act the age you want to be treated.

When this "Do" first hit me, I immediately thought "Cool! I'm going to act 75!"

Why not? Senior citizens get a lot of slack. A granny can look you in the eye and say, "Why in God's name would you stick that safety pin in your navel?" and all you can do is laugh. They also get into movies more cheaply, by the way.

It does make sense that if you act more mature, your parents might stop treating you like a day-care dropout. When I was in junior high, I sometimes found myself wondering just how I was supposed to act. There was no handbook that I could find at the time. It's just a weird stage. You start to look more like an adult, so your parents begin to expect you to do more adult things.

You see this teen confusion in girls in their early teens. One day their bedrooms arc onc big Barbic Bazaar, and then all of a sudden there's a hormonal surge and the entire décor is transformed into the Holy Shrine of the Backstreet Boys.

That stuff scares parents. They make cracks about their Jekyll-and-Hyde teens. It's scary for us too, of course. They say, "Act your age," and I'm thinking, "I'm 13. What do you want, a smoking jacket with a silk cravat?"

Truth be known, I was an Adult Talker at an early age. I'm the first-born son in my family, and I shadowed my dad as a kid, going to his seminars and conferences. There weren't many other kids around, so I had to learn to deal with adults. By the time I was ten, I spoke fluent Adult. Here's a sample: "Why, hello sir, how's the golf game?"

The adults seemed to appreciate that I could communicate on their level. It got me a lot of extra Cokes even though other kids were always being told, "Too much sugar will make you hyper." And it works for me even today. Right, Dad?

8. Be your own person.

This one should ring a few bells. It's the old "If Jimmy jumps off a bridge, are you going to jump too?" thing. Still, it doesn't hurt to be reminded because teens tend to run in packs. (Wild dogs, we are a bunch of wild dogs.) Like most teens, I got that peer-pressure junk in high school: *C'mon, smoke this. Drink that. What are you, a mama's boy? You're a puss if you don't sneak out tonight!*

Teenage manipulators lay big cons on you to get you to do their dirty work. Say one of your buddies on the football team wants to drive to Juarez and score some Bohemia beer, but he doesn't have a car. So he tries to con you into getting your parents' car so he can get beer. Bad deal.

Work this one out in a worst-case scenario. Your football buddy goes over the border in your parents' car. He buys the beer. Then gets busted over there. Your parents' car is impounded by the Mexican police. We're talking an international incident. And you're going to need U.N. armed forces to keep your parents from staging a public execution.

115

You have to learn to deal with peer pressure by rising above it and following your own values—not the wild pack's. A friend of my father's found out that his straight-A, soccer-star son was being taunted by some tough-guy degenerates on the high school bus. They were making fun of him for getting good grades, not smoking with them, and being an athlete. When the son told him, the dad gave him this mental image to carry on the next bus ride: "The next time they give you a hard time, look at them and picture where they'll be in twenty years. Then picture where you'll be in twenty years. They'll be the guys valet parking your car, son. They aren't cool. They're already lost, and they know it. That's why they resent you. They're nothing but scenery in your life. Just look at those losers and smile, because in twenty years, they'll be dogging you for a tip."

I like that better than the whole bridge-jumping scenario, don't you?

9. Look before you leap, but do leap.

Every parent wants his teen to live life to the fullest. Good parents work hard to give you the tools. But sometimes parents fall short. They screw up too. They don't always get the job done. They don't always get the message across. This book is an attempt to fill in the gaps.

Fear is the only thing that can keep you out of the big dance. If you aren't afraid to take risks, you'll be on that floor. You may fall on your keister once, twice, a dozen times. But when the music starts to fade, you'll never be ashamed of trying. It takes guts to get out there. It takes brains to decide whether the return is worth the risk.

The time to take well-considered risks is coming. Once you're out of school and on your own without a mortgage or a family to support, you'll be free to take on life. No fear! If you fall on your face, it won't be a big deal. Nobody with any sense is going to fault you for chasing your dream. So get into practice now by taking some risks. Go out for the football team. Run for student council. Ask that Penelope Cruz–looking babe if she'd like help with her chemistry. Dare life to slap you down. If it does, so what? Better to fail than to wake up at 50 and wonder why the hell you didn't give it a try when you had the chance.

Enough with the Teen Dos, let's get to the dark side: the Don'ts.

The Don'ts List

1. Don't be disloyal to your family.

What happens in your house stays in your house. It hurts everyone, including you, to go spouting off to your friends that "My dad is a total idiot!" or "My stepmom is a bitch!" First of all, what does that do to *your* reputation? Do your friends think you're a cool dude when you dis your own family? No, they're thinking they can't trust any of *their* secrets with you. They're also thinking that if your family is *that* zoned out, you must be a loser too! And what happens when your family finds out you've been publicly poor-mouthing them? Sooner or later, you'll be at a place in life when your family is all you've got. They'll open the door to you—but not if you've been peeing all over the porch!

Keep in mind too that when you air family problems in public, the outsiders are hearing only the *bad* news. They don't hear about it when your parents work things out. You're putting a bad rap on your family that will stick even when things turn around—and when they look bad, you look bad.

117

2. Don't lump all parents together, especially stepparents.

You don't like to be called a "typical teen." It's unfair. So give your parents a break. Look at them as individuals trying to do the right thing, in their own inept way. Stepparents deserve a stepbreak. Walking into a family-in-progress is no easy deal. They feel like strangers in the house. Wicked Stepparents. Give them a chance to prove themselves—and a little time to do it.

You can't develop a relationship with a stereotype. Lose the "Parents are all the same" attitude and give them the opportunity to succeed.

3. Don't blame your parents for your behavior.

They make me so mad. They made me run away. They made me get in trouble. What you do and how you respond to things are *your* responsibility. When you blame your parents, you give them too much credit. They might wish they could control your every action, but they can't.

You have unlimited options in how to respond to things that impact your life. Things happen *to* you. How you respond happens *within* you. So don't play the blame game.

4. Don't get mad at your parents when you know damn well they're right.

I had a girlfriend who threw tantrums that registered 9 on the Richter scale. She got some kind of perverse pleasure out of it. She was a drama queen. One time her friends decided to get tattooed to signify their membership in some little club they'd put together. Come to think of it, it might have been the Tantrum Club. It was an initiation thing. My girlfriend told her little buddy that she wanted one too. On her butt.

I knew she didn't really want to do it. She was scared to death of any kind of needle. And she thought tattoos were tacky. So she used her parents as a cover. With her friends present, she asked them if she could do it. She knew what they'd say. They told her she'd lost her mind.

I could see her smile to herself when they shot down the idea. But she threw one of her patented tantrums anyway. And I thought to myself: *Time for a new girlfriend.*

5. Don't be scared to ask for help.

I was trying to learn to drive a stick shift during driver's ed when my teacher told me to put it into high. I had no idea what he was talking about. High what? But I didn't want to seem uncool. So I shoved the stick shift as far forward as it would go. The grinding gears sounded like a train wreck. My attempt to be cool was canned.

Just as 99 percent of the male population refuses to ask directions, teens get into a lot of trouble that could be avoided if they'd just ask for help. The fear of appearing uncool or uninformed is a powerful force. Get over it. It's better to ask a question and have someone think you *might* be stupid than not to ask a question and *prove* that you're stupid.

6. Don't mistake your parents for fools.

A guy in my high school blew off class for a week, hung out with some dopers, and got high. After the school sent a notice about his absences to his parents, he tried to tell them that the school's computer was screwed up and that he'd really been there every day. He was a bad excuse maker but a decent actor. He put on this show of outrage and righteous indignation. His parents said, "Nice try," and grounded him until Britney Spears turns 30.

They may not know a CD-ROM from a DVD, but your parents don't deserve to be treated like global village idiots. I was giving a presentation in a high school class when I noticed a lot of sneaky stuff going on. People were whispering, passing notes, throwing things at each other. I was standing. They were sitting. So I could see everything. I began to wonder if the teacher was blind. Later, I asked her if she saw all the things that were going on.

"I see them, but if I reacted to all of them I wouldn't get anything else done," she said. "Besides, it's an advantage for me. If the students think I'm so stupid that I can't see what they're doing, odds are I'll catch them when they do something really bad!"

Parents know most of our games. If you think you're getting away with something, think again.

7. Don't play one parent off the other.

Teen: Hey, Dad, Mom says she doesn't care if I have another frozen Snicker's. Okay?

Dad: If your mother says it's OK, it's OK with me.

119

Welcome to Parent Ping-Pong, a game of cunning and conniving. To play you have to be a sneak, a liar, and a manipulator. True management material. It seems like an innocent game, but it can get real ugly real fast. Soon you'll slide into telling one parent that the other is being mean to you—just to get something you want. One lie leads to another. Eventually you'll get caught, and you will lose the trust of both parents. Or stepparents. This game is particularly popular with the children of divorced couples. It's called "getting even."

Stay out of this game. You'll get busted, and you're likely to do some major damage to your parents' relationship. If things get bad enough, you'll have to move on to the Divorce Game. You don't want to do that.

8. Don't make promises you won't keep.

A good negotiation is an agreement to meet each other's needs. It's got to be a win-win. And the terms have to be clear to both sides, otherwise you are in for some hell on Earth. When you are negotiating an agreement between you and your parents, do not walk away from the (kitchen) table unless both of you are happy with the deal. If you have tricked them into getting what you want and they got screwed, the payback will be painful—for you.

9. Don't lie to yourself.

It's bad to lie to your parents, but it's worse to lie to yourself. If you have a drinking problem or you're out of your league with some sexual issue, don't lie to yourself about it. This is called denial. Take time to review your life and determine if you are getting what you want. Focus on what you are not getting and why.

One of the things separating us from apes—other than the bars on the cages—is our ability to reflect on our actions and measure them against our beliefs. If you lie to yourself, you're wasting that gift—so you're just a big ape.

No one else can help you until you make up your mind that you need assistance. If we play games with ourselves and refuse to acknowledge our mistakes and failings, we're no better than some animal that lives by instinct. Be honest when looking at your actions. Admit when you've hurt someone or been disrespectful to your parents. Apologize to them. Start your own healing by reconnecting with the people who can be of the greatest help to you.

ANGER MANAGEMENT 101

Jessica was just 12 years old when her parents divorced. Jessica's father, Tom, started dating Katie three months after the divorce was final. It was war at first sight.

There is no good time for divorce, but this was one of the worst possible times for Jessica. It's tough enough to go through puberty and junior high when your family is getting along. Having her family torn apart at this stage of her life left Jessica angry and bitter.

She blamed her father for the divorce. To get back at him, she lashed out at every opportunity. When he and Katie married, she became Jessica's primary target. Jessica criticized and yelled at Katie so much it became a habit. She blamed Katie for anything that went wrong with her friends, at school, or at home. Even when Katie bought her stepdaughter presents, cooked her dinner, or took her shopping, Jessica struck out at her at every opportunity. Tom tried to stand up for his new wife, but whenever he wasn't around, Jessica would go after her.

By the time Jessica was 16, she was in full-blown rebellion. She was sexually promiscuous and flaunted it. She smoked, drank, and did drugs with a wild crowd of teens. Her anger became explosive. She'd grown taller than Katie, and with her height advantage she tried to intimidate her stepmother physically. Katie was small but athletic and strong. She'd grown up with four brothers. She was not easily frightened.

The war between stepdaughter and stepmother had mostly been a war of words, but just after Jessica's seventeenth birthday, she flew into a rage over something Katie told her to do. She rushed at her stepmother, grabbed her by the throat, and pinned her against the wall. "I hate you and I want to kill you!" she shrieked.

Katie broke away easily enough, but that night, she packed her bags and left. She loved Tom, but she could no longer live in the same house as Jessica and her increasingly violent temper. The anger and bitterness were too much.

The teen-parent relationship is rarely a walk in the park, Jessica and Katie were stumbling through Hell. In this case, the divorce and Jessica's unrelenting anger over it were a huge burden on their teen-stepparent relationship. But even in normal teen-parent relationships there are often high drama, explosions of temper, shouting, and door slamming.

There are several factors that make teens' relationships with parents so loaded with explosive emotions. Some of them are biological. Some of them are societal. Some of them are parents' fault, not teens'. Anger can be a useful emotion when controlled and converted to positive energy. Michael Jordan was a wizard at using his anger as a performance-enhancing (all-natural) drug. You can learn to do the same thing, but first it helps to understand what you are dealing with.

Why is it so hard for teens and parents to get along? What makes our relationships so volatile? Here are some of the major factors that contribute to the cats-and-dogs nature of the parent-teen relationship.

• *Teens stick around longer now.* In earlier generations and in some other cultures even today, the early to mid-teen years marked the time for parents and their young-adult children to split. Girls were considered to be of marriageable age at 13. Boys left to start careers, higher education, and their own families by 15 or 16. In our culture, teens generally don't leave home until they graduate from high school at the age of 18. Their natural cravings for freedom and independence run up against parents' natural desire to control what goes on in their own households.

• *Our brains are morphing.* There is a neurological phase common to teens that begins to occur in girls at about 14 to 16 years of age and to boys around 16 to 18. At that point, the brain begins to grow, creating separations between certain nerve endings. It is theorized that the frontal lobes extend themselves. There are also hormonal shifts and some physical remodeling of the brain. (This explains the hammering in your head.)

The frontal lobes are considered to be the control centers of your powers of judgment and empathy—the ability to understand and become sensitive to other people's feelings. With their brain's capacity for judgment short-circuited, teens don't think much about the future. They're into the here and now. They tend to be self-centered and obsessed with their own problems. They have little fear of death. They get distracted easily.

There's good news too. At this transitional stage, teens get ripped. They have the energy of a small power plant, which is a pretty good description of their bodies. They burn calories like a wood stove burns twigs. Their strength and endurance are at peak levels of performance. Their sleep cycle frequently flip-flops, so that they'll sleep from 4 A.M. until 2 P.M. one day and from 3 P.M. until 5 A.M. another. Bed head occurs at all hours of the day!

• *Our parents are overwhelmed.* Having teens in the house often puts parents on the defensive. Mutiny hangs in the air with every garbage bag not taken out to the trash. The high energy level of teens wears on their older, less active parents. They don't burn calories as fast as teens do. They don't build muscle mass as fast. They aren't as limber. They don't recover as quickly from exercise or illness. They get sore, stiff, and cranky.

At this point, you're probably wondering how parents and teens get along at all. We really are different in nearly every way. We're two types of people experiencing two vastly different worlds, so we are bound to have conflicts. That's why it's so important to try and connect whenever possible, in whatever way possible.

Making a connection is not about controlling the relationship. It's not about being "right." This type of thinking only creates more conflict. You gain power in your relationships and your life when you master the ability to stay in control of your most powerful emotions, especially your anger.

Unless it is controlled, anger gets in the way. It isolates you. I don't know about you, but when I see someone throwing a temper tantrum, I want to get the hell away. It shoves people in the opposite direction even when the emotions behind it might arise from need. Ever notice how hard it is to hug someone who's trying to knife you?

Martial arts experts, who teach their students how to control anger as a positive force, say that anger or negative energy weakens you physically and emotionally. There are four major factors involved in understanding and controlling anger:

- Timing
- Forgiveness
- Reframing
- Memory tapes

Timing Is Everything

Everyone is on one cycle or another. Our energy level cycles up and down every day, but the cycle is different for each of us. The daily energy cycles are called circadian cycles. Some of us are active at 11 A.M. and barely awake at 11 P.M.; others are just waking up at 8 P.M. but ready for bed by 8 A.M.

These cycles don't care whether you have to catch a 6 A.M. flight or pull an all-nighter for a biology exam. They just do their thing. We have to figure out a way to do ours. This is why Starbucks is taking over the world.

These cycles affect your moods. If you try to reason with someone when he or she is at a high point in the energy cycle, you will get a strong response—maybe a kiss on the cheek, maybe a shove. With teenagers, everything is heightened because of "raging hormones." The highs are higher, the lows are lower.

You can't control the fluctuations in your energy level, but you can learn to understand where you are in your daily cycle. If you feel anger building up, you know that you're at a highly emotional point in your cycle. That's a good time to go work out. It's a bad time to discuss household chores with your mother.

Forgiveness Takes the Edge Off

I'm not trying to sound like the pope here, but the Anger Experts say that the simple act of forgiveness is the best way to defuse the sort of burning, volcanic anger that Jessica is carrying around. Forgiveness is a way of cleaning your emotional house. You sweep out all the crap that's cluttering up your life and making it difficult to move forward. Anger wears the hell out of you. All that boiling blood can't be good for a person, can it? You have to let it go if you want any chance for a new connection. How do you forgive somebody who has screwed up your life? Take ten minutes and imagine all the anger-related junk cluttering up your life. In your imagination, review each one, consider why you would ever want to hang on to it, and then mentally toss it in the trash can. It will never do you any good anyway.

You may not be able to immediately run up and hug the person you've been wanting to choke for six months. That's okay. Instead of focusing on that person, focus on moving on to things that your anger and emotional stress have kept you from doing. Anger is like a drug; you have to come down from it over time.

It is possible to forgive even those people who've done terrible things to you. You've probably heard about Nelson Mandela and how his ability to forgive his jailers in South Africa so impressed them that they eventually campaigned for his release. I have an example closer to home. I know a teen whose mother accidentally shot off his arm when she was drunk. He has every reason to be angry with her, even to hate her. He could prey upon her guilt and drive her insane with his anger.

Instead, he chose to forgive her. He let it go. His forgiveness inspired his mother to quit drinking. They reconnected and now have a great relationship. If he can forgive his mother for the terrible thing she did to him, can't you practice some forgiveness too?

The first step in forgiveness is to simply let your anger go. Bitterness and anger don't do you any good. By forgiving your parents, you free yourself. If you can't do it for them, do it for yourself. If you let what they did to you ruin your life, then they've won. Don't let that happen.

Reframing Life to Be What You Want

My dad's friend Dave came home after driving a couple hundred miles for work and found his kid's bicycles, Hot Wheels, and other toys blocking the driveway. He was tired and hot. Disgusted with his kids for not putting their things away, he got out of his car and started clearing a path to his garage.

His neighbor, who was nearing retirement age and had just sent his youngest daughter off on her honeymoon, walked out of his house and watched Dave as he put the bikes away.

"Enjoy it while you can," the neighbor said. "They're gone before you know it."

That one sentence immediately changed Dave's attitude. His disgust and anger disappeared. The mess made by his kids was no longer a pain in the ass. It was a gift. "As long as there are bikes cluttering the driveway, I'll still have kids around," he thought.

He never again got upset when the driveway was blocked.

The neighbor's words caused Dave to "reframe" the situation. It was as if he could suddenly see a picture of the cluttered driveway from an entirely different perspective. It was definitely a much longer-range view. He had been focusing on himself and the short-term inconvenience of having to get out of the car and clean up the mess. His neighbor made him step back and appreciate the stage of life he was in, with his children still around to enjoy. He realized that his anger was silly. That was all it took.

The process of reframing your perspective—as accomplished by Dave in the driveway—is a wonderful tool for tossing out the wasted energy of anger. He did it unconsciously in that case, but after that, he taught himself to do it whenever he felt anger creeping up on him. He did it by thinking about a framed illustration hanging on a wall in his house. Up close, it looks like a modernistic painting with random splashes of color, but when you back away from it twenty feet or so, you can distinguish a face and other figures. The farther you get from the illustration, the more clearly you can make out the real meaning of the print.

He learned to do the same with his anger, by slowly moving away mentally and emotionally from the situation that had raised his blood pressure and reframing it with the longer-range perspective. The next time you get angry with your parents, for whatever reason, try reframing that anger. Step back and take the long view. Is it worth so much of your energy to stay angry? Wouldn't it be better to forgive your parents and reconnect with them so that you can enjoy the long-term benefits of a good relationship?

Anger on Tape

Curtis had a problem doing any kind of handy work around the house. Whether it was putting together shelving, assembling a swing set, or changing the fuses in his car, he'd always find himself rushing through the task as if he had to get it done immediately. Even when there was no rush, he'd become stressed out, agitated, and angry.

Finally it dawned on him that he was hearing his father's voice in his mind. When he was a teenager, Curtis had tried to help his dad, who was a skilled handyman. He could fix anything, but he had no patience with his son. He'd yell at Curtis instead of teaching him how to do things: "Hurry up with that, dammit!"

Curtis carried the tape of those stressful experiences with his father in his mind. He unconsciously played that tape while doing chores as an adult, and it triggered stressful feelings and anger long after his father was gone from his life.

129

Most people have similar "tapes" playing in a continuous loop through their lives. Some are pleasant, others are not. These memory tapes can be destructive because a lot of times we are not even consciously aware of them. Yet they can trigger powerful emotions and strong reactions.

Julia is one of the sweetest ladies you will ever meet, but her emotionally charged memory tapes made her life miserable. We had a psychology class together in high school. One day we were supposed to give a presentation together. As we were preparing, I overheard her talking to herself: "I will make a fool of myself. I can't do it. I can't do it." She talked herself out of making the presentation, and she had to take a failing grade on it, which ruined her A average in the class.

Memory tapes can sabotage your life and your relationships. The girl who tells you "I've been burned before" is running an unpleasant memory tape in her head. You can't live out of your memory. You have to look forward. Nobody drives a car while looking in the rearview mirror constantly. You have to look ahead to move ahead.

The Physical Effects of Anger

Anger and stress create a chemical imbalance in the body and mind. The scientific name for this is "being pissed off."

Made you laugh, didn't I?

Humor is a relief for the physical effects of anger and stress. So the next time somebody's joking around while you're mad, consider the humor to be an anger antidote. When a person gets stressed, her breathing becomes more shallow. There's not as much oxygen available to the brain or muscles. It's been shown that you lose about 15 IQ points when you are stressed for more than fifteen minutes. Angry and stupid—now that's a formula for disaster.

Your muscles lose 3 percent of their strength during stress. Have you ever watched Olympic athletes do deep breathing before an event? They are strengthening themselves. It has been shown that students can increase their grades if they do breathing exercises, because they can remember things better and have greater logical power. The shallow breathing that takes place during stress has been found to trigger feelings of depression because the brain becomes depleted of oxygen. It doesn't seem fair that the happier you are, the smarter you are, does it? Wouldn't it be better if as you got more depressed you got smarter, so that you could figure out how to be happier? Nature screws up again.

Stress also robs you of pain-relieving neurotransmitters. You get more headaches and more back pain. I practice martial arts to relieve stress and anger. One of the key principles of martial arts is to "center" your mind and body and focus on what you need to do to perform at your best. When you learn to clear your thoughts and emotions in this way, events and people cannot throw you off balance so easily.

Breathing Techniques

I want to get it on the record here and now that I've always been a *huge* proponent of breathing, except underwater, of course. Breathing is a way of life for me. It's like oxygen. But we're talking about special breathing techniques that restore the oxygen and boost the fuel to your mind and body. One of the most effective methods of calming your anger and restoring balance is to breathe in a controlled pattern. This technique has been around for centuries. The goal is to breathe out for the same amount of time as you breathe in. I was taught at first to count to seven as I exhaled and then to seven when I inhaled, repeating the pattern again and again.

When you try this, you realize that you tend to inhale more than you exhale. This is the way you breathe when you get stressed, only worse. When you take in more air than you breathe out, you tend to hyperventilate. This is not good. You develop an imbalance of oxygen in your body, which stimulates muscle spasms, and that creates imbalance in your mind.

The breathing techniques I follow are relatively easy. Once you

131

make them a habit, they become a very good tool for keeping your cool during stressful situations. If the situation involves someone wanting to take you apart limb by limb, it can also make that person think you are:

1. A martial arts master with deadly skills
2. Crazed and dangerous
3. About to pass out from fear and therefore not worth punching

Centering Yourself

This chapter is beginning to go Bruce Lee on us, but I want to give you at least one more technique for keeping nasty old Mr. Anger out of your life. It is the martial arts technique of "centering." Normally when we walk around, the weight balance of our bodies is around our belly button. For those of you with pot bellies, this explains all those scars on your forehead.

Good athletes often center themselves unconsciously during competition. My basketball coach used to talk about "squaring up" to the basket, which is a method of getting your body in position and in balance so you can shoot.

Interestingly, if you are engaging in a battle of wits, you tend to center your balance around the brain. Observe people as they enter an important business meeting. Watch lawyers enter a courtroom. Most look as if they could fall over headfirst. They walk with their heads out in front of their bodies—leading with their brains.

In physical activity, it's best to keep your balance around your lower trunk so that it's hard to knock you down or move you. Football linemen are good at shifting their center of balance lower to the ground. Weight lifters talk about "building a base" by lowering their centers of gravity before a lift. Gymnasts always know where their center of gravity lies. When you move your balance down to your lower trunk, you arc more secure and balanced.

What's this got to do with Anger Management 101? The way you live in your body affects how you live in the world. If you are not balanced physically, you will not be balanced psychologically. If you are balanced psychologically, you can control your anger and restore balance to your life and relationships.

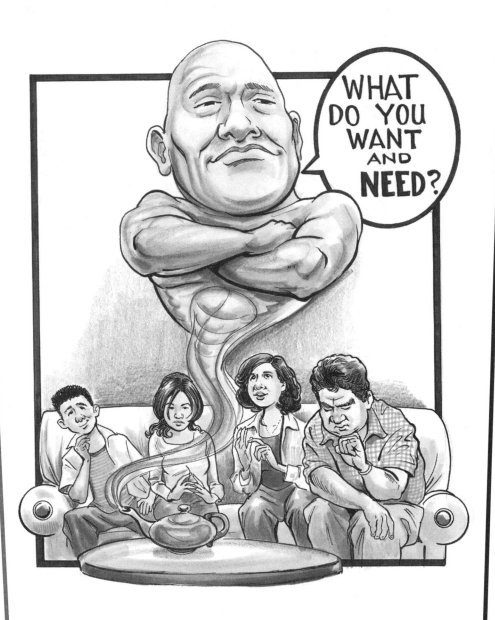

10

THE FORMULA FOR RECONNECTING PARENTS AND TEENS

Travis was the golden boy of his high school class in an affluent community out West. He was a good-looking kid, athletic, popular, and smart. He lived in an upper-middle-class neighborhood with his mother, father and sister. Both parents worked. His father traveled a lot in his sales job. As far as anyone knew, Travis was a happy kid with a bright future.

His family, friends, neighbors, and classmates were stunned when he was arrested and charged with aggravated assault and burglary in the summer after his senior year. But they were knocked out when the local newspaper reported that he had committed his violent crime as part of his initiation into the Latin Disciples street gang.

Police officers from the gang unit said the street gang had moved into the community from Los Angeles. Its leaders were working to expand the gang's influence beyond urban areas. They recruited non-Hispanic teens by providing them with cash, drugs, and girls. It had been easier to lure them in than the gang had expected.

With both parents and his sister working, Travis had found himself home alone a lot that summer. He'd met the gang recruiters at a city park while playing basketball. Travis had a wide circle of friends, but these Hispanic guys from the barrio with their low-riding cars and secretive ways made him feel cool and a little dangerous. He'd never been around guys who seemed to care so much about each other. They were constantly talking about how much they loved each other and how they were dedicated to watching each other's backs and protecting each other. He'd never heard that kind of talk from his friends.

The gang members told Travis that he was the coolest white guy they'd ever met. They asked him to become the first Anglo to be a member of their gang. For his initiation, he had to break into a neighbor's house and steal at least $5,000 worth of cash, electronic equipment, jewelry, whatever he could get. His new best friends said they'd be watching his back from a van parked outside.

Travis didn't see the 70-year-old woman until she hit him on the shoulder with a golf club. It glanced off, but he instinctively threw a punch in the direction of the blow. He shattered the bones on one side of her face. She'd already called 911 after hearing glass break on a downstairs window. A police officer caught Travis as he came running out of the woman's garage. The friends who were supposed to be watching his back were long gone.

Travis went to prison on a fifteen-year sentence. The judge said he hoped it would be a lesson to anyone in the community tempted to join a street gang. When Travis's distraught parents asked the police gang crimes officer why their bright and popular son would ever be persuaded to join a gang, his answer was this: "They obviously filled a need that wasn't being filled for him anywhere else."

Whether you are talking about your dealings with your parents, your teen, or your friends, all of your relationships are based on one common characteristic: they fill a need. When one of the parties in a relationship isn't getting his or her needs fulfilled, that relationship disintegrates and the person goes looking somewhere else to have those needs fulfilled.

Teenagers are needy. They especially need to feel a sense of belonging and acceptance. Gang leaders are needy too. They need members to do their dirty work. And they're cunning when it comes to meeting the needs of teens to draw them in. They're masters of street psychology. They lure teens in by providing whatever needs are not being met by their families. Their members will rob and murder, accept beatings, and even kill themselves out of loyalty to fellow gang members.

In Chicago several years ago, Big Red, a leader of the Latin Kings, was released from prison. When he got out, he discovered that his old gang had hooked up with a larger gang. He couldn't believe it. He was so distraught about what had happened to his "family" that he walked into the street, pointed a double-barreled shotgun under his jaw, and said, "Tell the Kings this is what I died for." He then pulled the trigger.

Gang members are often sociopaths, but they understand the social needs of teenagers. They realize that we are an interdependent species. We need to belong to something greater than ourselves. It's how we survived and flourished in the reality version of *Jurassic Park*. It is how we built a complex society. It's how we built Dave & Buster's and a Ronald McDonald empire that now rules the world . . . okay, I'm over it.

Every relationship you have is based on your needs and the needs of the other person. In the remaining chapters, I will help you examine your parent-teen relationship. We'll study it from every angle and determine how to make it the best and strongest relationship in your life.

I can give you guidance and some very useful tools, but the only person who can make your relationship work is you. Parents can dictate to their teens, but they can't change them. Teens can rebel and manipulate their parents, but they can't change them either. The only thing you can do is change yourself and hope that your efforts will inspire a more positive response from the other side.

As you approach relationships, you have to think, "What can I do to make this relationship better?" and then put all of your focus on that. If your approach to reconnecting with your parent or teen is to say, "What you need to do . . ." then you just hit their mute button. They can see your jaws flapping, but they don't hear a word you're saying. Command and control are not an option in this scenario.

You have to work on yourself first, then lead by example. You can't think of yourself as the leader in the relationship reconstruction. You have to think of yourself as "the connector." There is a universal formula for success in a parent-teen relationship. And that formula is this:

The quality of a relationship is the extent to which it meets the deepest needs of the people involved.

If you're entangled in a messed-up relationship with your teen, you are not meeting his or her needs. If you have a poor relationship with your parents, either you're not meeting their needs or they aren't meeting yours.

It's got to be a two-way street, the whole Three Musketeers thing. All for one and one for all. If your teen doesn't respond to your attention and affection with her own efforts to reach out to you, the formula won't work. Sooner or later, you will disconnect again.

In the chapters that follow, I'm going to show you how to reconnect and stay connected to your parents or teen. Here's a quick rundown of what we'll be doing in the rest of the book.

No matter how bad your relationship has become, even if it's gotten to the neck-grabbing, name-calling bottom of the barrel, it's not impossible to fix it. But you have to make fixing it a priority. Your Mission Impossible assignment. So, Mr. and Ms. Phelps, here is your mission.

There are four tasks that must be done to pull it off. None of them, by the way, involves hanging upside down from a helicopter going 240 miles per hour five feet off the surface of a flowing river of lava.

Mission Step No. 1:

Decide what you want out of the relationship and why.

That might be harder to determine than you think. If I handed you Aladdin's lamp right now, what would you tell the genie if he popped out and offered to fulfill any wish? (Careful, this is a family-oriented parent-teen manual.)

Most people have trouble giving a quick answer that isn't a joke. They'll say they don't really know what they want. But if one of their basic needs is not being met, you can be sure they'll sense that something is wrong. To get your parent-teen relationship back on track, you will have to determine exactly what it is you want. If you can't identify it, how can anyone else? You are going to have to look inside yourself, maybe for the first time, and ask, "What do I want from them? What will it take to make me happy, secure, and fulfilled?"

Mission Step No. 2:

Share your needs.

You can't expect people to read your mind. You have to teach people what you need. If they love you, if they're devoted to your success, if they really don't hate you even though you may think they do, there's hope for your relationship. If you give them a connect-the-dots map to what makes you a happy person, they just might help out. But you have to make your needs known.

One thing to remember before we get started: you're going to have to go a little deeper than those "needs" that rise up every time you walk into Best Buy, Old Navy, or Fast Charlie's Chevrolet dealership.

Typically, if you ask your teen, "What do you want?," he replies, "A new Corvette."

"Oh, really? And how would you feel if you had a new Corvette?"

"I would be Testosterone Boy. I can just see myself pulling into that parking lot at school and all the babes running over to check me out."

There is a need being expressed, but it doesn't lie beneath the hood of the Corvette. You have to move beneath the superficial expression of his need to be the center of female attention. He's talking about feeling proud of a possession. He wants to be recognized. Maybe even loved and valued.

To get reconnected to your parents or teen, you have to expose that raw, beating need. *What do you need?* "I want my parents to get off my ass!" "I want to have a chance to be with my friends!" What true needs are being expressed there? Here's the translation: "I want a sense of belonging. I want a sense of independence. I want a sense of self-direction." All those things are good to want. No parent would argue with that.

If you sit down with your parents and say, "I want to be with my friends more and have you get off my back," that's not going to sell

139

very well, as opposed to saying "I really feel a need to have some independent life. I don't want to be away from you, but I want some separation, I want some individuality, I want some trust from you so I can have some confidence in myself."

When you can express your needs from an *internal* frame of reference that makes those needs your personal responsibility, you let the other person off the hook in terms of giving or buying you something. Expressing your deepest needs opens the door for them. It makes it far easier to reconnect.

Mission Step No. 3:

Find out their needs.

Next, you have to work to discover the needs of your partner. Teens or parents, this means that you have to get outside yourself long enough to say, "You know, I've been so focused on controlling Jimmy that I haven't focused on understanding his point of view. What makes him tick? What is he interested in? What does he want and need from me?"

A quick side note here, Mr. and Ms. Phelps: As your mission unfolds, you'll notice something interesting: if you're working to make your needs known and your relationship target partner is looking to discover your needs, this could all work out pretty well, don't you think?

This is all about closing the gap that's grown between you. It's about discovering each other and appreciating each other again. If you both stay focused on this mission, you will find each other as you are right now. The past is done. Parents will be amazed to find that you've outgrown both the Ninja Turtles *and* the Power Rangers and that you no longer want to be a superhero when you grow up. They may even recognize that you are on the edge of adulthood and deserve to be taken seriously.

Parents, you never know when you will meet the most exciting, intriguing, inspiring person you've ever encountered. That might be the teen in your home right now. What if you discover that your teen's likes and wants and needs are deeply felt, well conceived, and inspiring? You may find the pot of gold: pride in your teen.

Mission Step No. 4:

Work out a plan for reconnecting.

Once you've each identified what you need from the relationship and then made those needs known to each other, it's time to come up with a plan.

This part of the mission isn't so impossible. Every need that you've identified can be a step or objective. If you want support from your parents, be supportive of them. If you want respect from your teen, be respectful of her. If you want a good relationship partner, you've got to be one yourself first.

This part of the mission is all about negotiating a win-win so that both sides have their needs met by the other. Sound easy? I'm not going to lie. At some point, you just might feel as if you *are* hanging upside down from a helicopter over a hot river of lava. Some of those old simmering hurts and resentments may come boiling up during these negotiations. That's not necessarily bad. You may need to blow off a last blast of steam. But there are ways to do it and not destroy the negotiation process.

Most people don't get what they want because they lack certain basic negotiation skills that work in almost any situation, whether you are negotiating with union bosses, a car salesman, or your parents. Once again, your full-service parent-teen relationship guru presents those negotiation skills to you at no extra charge. However, tips *are* accepted.

141

Rules of Negotiation

1. Know what you really want, and focus on that. Make it no more than two things; one is even better. As a teen, you may want to stay with a friend overnight on Saturday, you may want to buy a new dress

for a Friday-night special event, you may want the car on Sunday. That's too much to work with all at once, and the danger is that if there are too many things you want, all of them become negotiable. If you want to do A, then you cannot do B and C. Be flexible and remember to know what you need, rather than what you want.

2. Find out what the other person wants. Delve deeply into the needs the person has, and try to be creative in finding ways to meet them. For example, if he or she wants you to be safe and secure, consider ways of keeping in contact. This is the creative part of negotiation, but the most challenging. Keep an open mind.

3. Work out a deal. With clear action plans and objectives, agree on what actions each of you is going to perform and what results you expect from the other. You might want to write this down or even videotape it. *There must be a clear, specific understanding.* Again, don't make it complicated. Simply state: If you do A and B, then you will get C and D.

I will give you more tips on how to put your action plan into place in Chapter 13. This negotiation step is critical to the success of your mission. It's the final scene in which you enter the lair of the bad guys, get the girl (or guy) back, and shut down the nuclear missile launch. Pretty exciting, huh?

Of course, your mission is more personal than saving the planet: you want to save your relationship with your teen or parent. You want to reconnect because, let's face it, who wants to go to family reunions for the next forty years and listen to a lot of screaming and fighting?

If you want to reconnect with your teens, if you want your teens to reconnect with you, start connecting the dots.

Special Instructions for Blended Families

If people think it's tough being a teen, try being a stepteen. The same holds true for parents and stepparents. Stepteens and stepparents are notoriously hard on each other. It's not only you. You've been placed in a difficult and challenging situation just by the nature of the circumstances. You don't have those natural paternal and maternal bonds working for you. You haven't had a lifetime to learn how to communicate with each other. Often you've come together after a traumatic period. There is bound to be some conflict.

It helps to recognize the situation, and to understand the perspective of the other side.

There are always hassles and jealousies in blended families that don't exist in boring old traditional families. One side thinks you favor the other. The other side thinks you have abandoned them. Kids will play one parent off the other. Parents will trip all over themselves trying to hide their biases. You have to listen to each other and recognize each other's needs. You have to communicate your needs to each other. A stepfather has to say things like "I want harmony. I'm not trying to be your dad. But we are coexisting, and I am in a position of responsibility. I have to make some hard decisions, and we have to negotiate some things so we can get along and grow together."

It's amazing how well a little communication works! Tell your stepkids and your stepparents what you need to feel secure and comfortable and wanted. Listen to their needs too. Work together to build win-win situations. They'll come to your soccer games, and you'll go to dinner with them afterward. You'll baby-sit the younger kids, and they'll pay you so you can get those CDs you've been wanting.

143

Whatever type of family situation you're in, if you follow the Mission Steps I've given you, you'll find that the formula works. Parents need to have a plan. They need to find effective ways of deepening their relationship with their teens. They need to find creative ways of showing their love for them. And teens need to know how to get what they want by negotiating with their parents instead of sneaking around them. To make this work, you have to go through it yourself. You have to be the writer of your own script because you know your needs better than anyone else.

DISCOVERING YOUR NEEDS

To quote the ancient British philosopher Mick Jagger, "You can't always get what you want, but if you try sometimes you just might find you get what you need."

What Mick means is that we often confuse wants with needs. You might think that happiness will come with a ten-thousand-watt stereo or a Mustang Cobra GT but what you really want is to be noticed, appreciated and—getting down to the real thang—loved.

A good relationship is one in which both sides feel fulfilled. Your best friend fulfills your need to be admired for your sense of humor. You fulfill his need to have someone who shares his interest in college football. If he decides you really aren't that funny, or if you decide college football is overhyped, the relationship will likely fall apart. Both sides have to get something and put something in.

If your parent-teen relationship is in a rut or on the rocks, it is because the needs and expectations for the relationship are going unmet. Maybe the teen feels that she isn't getting enough understanding from her mother. Maybe a parent feels that he is not respected. There's a gap somewhere. Our mission is to figure out where it is and then close it. But first you have to figure out what it is that floats your boat. What are your needs?

The constant consumer hype to get this and buy that confuses us.

We become convinced that things can satisfy our most important needs. But did you ever get something you thought you really, really, really wanted and then feel a sense of being let down when you got it? Odds are you were looking for more than that mere thing could provide. You thought it would bring you instant happiness, but once again you'd mistaken a superficial *want* for a much deeper *need*.

You don't have to feel like the Lone Ranger. It happens to everybody. Most people can't articulate their needs, but they know when they aren't being fulfilled. It's like you don't know there is a hole in your pants until a little blast of wind hits exposed flesh. Something isn't covered. Something's missing. You feel emptiness or an ache.

When you find yourself feeling depressed, stuck, or a little psycho, it's usually because there's a need in your life that is going unmet. It could be a lack of security in a relationship or a lack of creative expression. Often, it's a lack of love.

It can be freaky to look within yourself for what is missing and causing that dull ache. You might discover some need that you fear will never be satisfied. A teen told me one time that she hoped she would never fall in love because she'd probably never get it to last. "If I never experience love, I'll never know what I missed," she said.

That's not much of a way to live. You can't insulate yourself from your feelings and needs. They are too much a part of us. Before you can start to reconnect with your parent or teen, you need to determine what your needs are. After all, you can't tell anyone else what's missing from your life if you haven't figured it out yourself, right?

Profiling Your Needs

We're about to get down to the nitty-gritty. This exercise is designed to help you identify your needs. To do so successfully, you have to be open about your feelings. Those of us who are not Oprah aren't real good at that. Guys especially. But you have to approach this exercise without resentment or fear. There's no need to justify or explain why you feel the way you feel. There's no reason to think that you're crazy or neurotic. This is just a way of finding out the depth of your true feelings and needs. There are no right needs or wrong needs, just your needs.

Figuring Out What You Want

We're going needs shopping. Time to check the shelves and pantry of your heart and soul. What's missing? Make a list of those needs that you feel are not being met by your parents or your teenager. Include things that you desperately want as well as those that you fantasize about. I have included some questions to help you get started, but add more if you'd like. As you list them, consider how many of these apparent needs can be met and in what ways they can be met by your family.

1. What things do you think you need (cars, clothes, etc.)?
2. What privileges do you think you need (curfew extension, food, money, etc.)?
3. What titles do you think you need (best, prettiest, president, boss, fastest, etc.)?
4. What roles or jobs do you think you need (boss, supervisor, chief, mother, father, etc.)?
5. What relationships do you think you need (dating the football hero, being best friends with the boss, belonging to the best club, etc.)?
6. What economic needs do you have (money, security, house, etc.)?
7. What jobs do you think you need (doctor, artist, teacher, a steady job, etc.)?
8. What situations do you feel you need to control (family, school, job, etc.)?

147

9. What condition of your life do you need changed (more peace and quiet, more stimulation, etc.)?

10. _____

11. _____

12. _____

13. _____

14. _____

15. _____

Basic Needs Assessment

Most people get confused about their needs because they think they can be satisfied by material things. We are told by advertisements and marketing experts to spend our money on their products to satisfy our basic needs. Can you believe we buy into that baloney? How else could we get conned into spending $45,000 for a convertible BMW because we think it will bring us prestige, respect, and attention? Buy a Bud at the bar and beautiful women will fall all over you? Is it working for you, big guy?

When you fall into the materialistic mentality, you end up with a full house but an empty heart. The Mitsubishi big-screen television won't do it. The Ralph Lauren leather couch won't either. You could buy out Neiman-Marcus and Nordstrom, and you'd still have to deal with that nagging feeling that there has to be more to life. There is more to life, but you can't put it on your charge card or make easy monthly payments to get it.

Again, you are confusing wants and true needs that are tied closely to your quality of life. Until you recognize your basic needs, you can never figure out how to meet them. The needs that add real value to our lives can be generally classified as those related to:

- Belonging
- Security
- Self-esteem
- Vocational or artistic expression
- Love and affection

You may think of more categories than I've come up with. I thought about giving Dairy Queen Oreo Blizzards their own "needs" category, but my editor, who is probably a yogurt lover, ruled it out.

This isn't an exact science like horticulture. It's more like chiropractic. We're trying to feel around and find out what hurts so we can make a few adjustments and ease the pain in your life. It's going to take a few minutes of examination. Fortunately, we make house calls.

Note that some needs fit under more than one category. The need to feel special, for instance, could be considered both a need for self-esteem and a need for affection. Take each category in the lists below and check off the basic needs that you think are addressed. For example, buying a BMW convertible is a "want" that attempts to meet a more basic need for recognition, status, or windblown hair. Make a list of the "wants" you named and make another list under each one of the basic needs that you think they are an attempt to fulfill. Check off all the needs you feel now, both the ones you think are being met and the ones you feel are not being met.

149

Safety and Physical Needs

1. ( ) The need to know that my family is safe physically
2. ( ) The need to know that my family is safe from psychological or social harm
3. ( ) The need to be touched as a sign of support, care, and approval
4. ( ) The need to feel physically welcomed with a hug, a handshake, a kiss, or a pat on the back
5. ( ) The need to have appropriate clothing for my situation

6. ( ) The need to have transportation and ways of getting to places
7. ( ) The need to feel safe from physical abuse
8. ( ) The need to feel safe from abusive psychological behavior
9. ( ) The need to have a place for reflection
10. ( ) The need not to suffer humiliation from my family
11. ( ) Others:

Belonging Needs

1. ( ) The need to feel a sense of belonging
2. ( ) The need to know I've been forgiven
3. ( ) The need to feel accepted with all my flaws and faults
4. ( ) The need to know I have close friends
5. ( ) The need for family connections
6. ( ) The need to feel welcome and wanted by my family
7. ( ) The need to be emotionally connected
8. ( ) The need to be part of a team
9. ( ) The need to be treated with courtesy and politeness
10. ( ) The need to share joy and fun
11. ( ) Others:

Security Needs

1. ( ) The need to be valued by my family
2. ( ) The need to be supported in times of distress, conflict, or embarrassment
3. ( ) The need to know that someone will rally to my side when he or she is needed
4. ( ) The need to know that I can get guidance when I am out of control and confused
5. ( ) The need to know that someone will protect me when I am threatened
6. ( ) The need to feel loyalty

7. (   ) The need to feel commitment
8. (   ) The need to know that I have a place to go when my world falls apart
9. (   ) The need for a relationship that will hold up regardless of disagreements or confrontations
10. (   ) The need for security
11. (   ) Others:

Self-Esteem Needs

1. (   ) The need to be respected
2. (   ) The need to be appreciated for my service to others
3. (   ) The need to feel important
4. (   ) The need to feel special
5. (   ) The need to feel that my family is proud of me
6. (   ) The need to be trusted to make good decisions
7. (   ) The need for appreciation
8. (   ) The need for nonverbal encouragement such as nods, smiles, high fives, etc.
9. (   ) The need to be proud of my accomplishments
10. (   ) The need to display and share my accomplishments
11. (   ) Others:

Vocational/Expression Needs

1. (   ) The need to explore my talents
2. (   ) The need to try new things
3. (   ) The need to express myself
4. (   ) The need to plan a career
5. (   ) The need to plan my marriage and family life
6. (   ) The need to explore lifestyle options
7. (   ) The need to focus on the demands of my vocation or special interests
8. (   ) The need to take responsibility for my life
9. (   ) The need to want something better in life

10. ( ) The need to use my talents and passions in my vocation
11. ( ) Others:

Affection Needs

1. ( ) The need to feel and be told that I'm loved
2. ( ) The need to feel needed
3. ( ) The need to feel that I am a priority in someone's life
4. ( ) The need to feel that I am special to someone
5. ( ) The need to feel that someone else takes pride in my accomplishments
6. ( ) The need to be heard
7. ( ) The need to be understood
8. ( ) The need to share joy and happiness with someone
9. ( ) The need to share sadness and depression with someone
10. ( ) The need to be wanted by someone
11. ( ) Others:

Evaluation of Basic Needs Assessment

You've identified your needs on the lists above. On those lists, give a rating of 0% to 100% for how each need is being met by your parents or your teen. For example, if you need to feel you are loved and your family is totally meeting this need, you'd put down 100%. Since we are discussing your parents or teen, you may want to be specific to that person in terms of how well he or she is meeting your needs. If you feel that a need is being met only halfway, put down 50%, and if you feel that none of that need is being fulfilled, put down 0%. (Anyone who puts down 31.5% will obviously be fulfilling a need to be a smart-ass.)

Need	Percentage Met by Family
1.	
2.	
3.	
4.	
5.	
6.	
7.	
8.	
9.	
10.	

The Last Step: Figuring Out What Needs Can Be Met by Others

You've been focusing on exploring your needs. If you've stuck with it so far, you are obviously committed to reconnecting with your parent or teen. Congratulations! You may already have gained some insights into your needs and how to satisfy them. You may also have come to the realization that it is unrealistic to expect others to meet needs that you've never expressed, unless of course, you have a direct connection to the Psychic Friends hot line.

All of us have needs. We discover them over a lifetime as we change and mature. It is not a sign of weakness to have them. It takes maturity to acknowledge that you rely on others for certain things. The better defined your needs are, the more effective you can be in bringing happiness in your life.

Frank was one of the smartest teens I have ever known, but he couldn't stay out of trouble. He welcomed it. He once stole a car, drove it to Denny's, and sat at the counter drinking coffee until the police invited him down to the station. Doughnuts were not part of the deal.

Frank was sabotaging his life. He aced most of his tests, but he'd toss his homework assignments out the window. His parents were on speed dial at the principal's office, the police station, and juvenile court. Time and time again, they were ordered to get Frank counseling before he self-destructed. They were cold fish. They didn't make any effort to get him help. Their response was "He'll grow out of it."

It bothered me that this likable, intelligent guy was so bent on throwing his life down the toiler. One day I blurted out, "Frank, you're the smartest person I know. Why are you always getting yourself in trouble? One of these days when you get a judge who doesn't care, he's going to send you up the river. Why do you want to do that?"

Frank smiled at me in the weirdest way before answering. It was the saddest smile I'd ever seen. Finally he said, "My parents expect me to be perfect. They take me for granted when I'm their good boy. But when I do something bad, they have to talk to me. It's the only way I can get any reaction from them."

He looked at me as if to let me know he was confiding in me. "You know what is so interesting? They will call me names and threaten me, but it doesn't hurt as much as being ignored. That hurts the most."

Frank told me that I was the first friend to confront him about his troublemaking, and he admitted that it had gone too far. He'd become addicted to the attention it was bringing from his parents, but he didn't really want to ruin his reputation. He thanked me for being a good friend.

The last I heard, Frank was in law school. It had taken him about three months to get his grade point average back up to 4.0. I think he turned in three months of homework in a week. He'd been doing it all along but stuffing it in a drawer. The only sad thing is that as far as I know, he never opened up to his parents the way he did to me. Maybe they never showed the same interest that I did.

Frank knew his needs, but he chose a messed-up way to make them known to his parents. Fortunately, he had strong instincts of self-preservation and they overcame his need for his parents' affection.

Further Study

I know that most people are not going to make a long-term study of their emotional needs. It can be exhausting, and there's always something good on HBO to distract you. I do suggest that you start a journal as an easy way to keep up on your needs and how they change. Writing is a tremendous form of self-therapy because when you write something down, you take it from a thought to an expressed idea that can be processed and studied anytime.

Take each category and write down the needs you've just identified and reviewed. Expand the description of your needs under this heading. For example, if emotional needs were your first category, write that category down and list all the things that you feel will fulfill you emotionally. Remember that these notes of yours are not to be shared with anyone at this time. These are only for your use.

Then go on to the next category. If security is the next category, write down what you want for your own security needs. The material is only a building block. It doesn't have to be consistent. It doesn't have to be logical. It only has to be written. Allow yourself to write whatever you feel.

For teens, it might be a little frustrating because you may not have all the words to express your feelings. It may take some time to explore why you sometimes feel unfulfilled in relationships, especially with your parents. Through this exercise, search your experiences to see if your frustrations arise when the needs you have identified are not fulfilled. You may discover new categories of needs in the process. The challenge is to find the words that express your feelings.

For parents this may be an opportunity to rediscover some of the dreams you've given up. It may be time for you to look deep into your history and identify unfulfilled needs in other relationships and define

155

them. This is not the time to play safe with your feelings. Don't be conservative in expressing your needs. Lay them out. They may have been buried, blunted, or frustrated a long time ago. You may not even be aware of the exact words you want to use. Don't let your fears control you during this exercise. So often we are silent about our needs because we are afraid. This exercise is your permission to reach inside your heart. This is to find out who you are.

Barriers to Awareness

Perhaps it would be helpful to figure out why you haven't been able to identify your needs up to this point. There are many reasons we neglect our dreams. There are four types of burdens on the parent-teen relationship. These are:

1. The broad and sweeping fear of rejection
2. The fear of inadequacy—physical, mental, or emotional
3. The fear of abandonment
4. The fear of disappointment

Assignment: In your journal, create a category of fears. This list includes all those fears and situations that tend to block expression of your needs. With as much detail and description as possible, list and describe all the situations you are afraid of. Really dig deep, and identify every fear and every limitation that disable you. Some of these fears may be rational, some irrational. If they are part of you, be honest and identify them.

Once you have completed this process, you can then begin to identify your fears and your needs more easily. You will feel better grounded, better balanced. You may also experience some sadness, anger, or frustration as you explore your feelings more fully. You may find some things that you've been repressing rather than dealing with. It's good to air those feelings instead of bottling them up.

DISCOVERING YOUR NEEDS

This chapter serves as a guide to exploring and recognizing our needs. Feel free to review it from time to time. I've given you this process for tuning in to needs that you may never have expressed or dealt with. Just doing that is a big step toward happiness. But we're not done yet, so stick with it. We're about to take a big leap over that gap in your parent-teen relationship.

12

TUNING IN TO THE NEEDS OF OTHERS

Pam was a girl who knew her needs. She wanted to be with the captain of the football team in the fall and the captain of the basketball team in the winter. She wanted to be the Homecoming Queen and head cheerleader as well as the hostess of every major party in the high school. You could say that her basic needs were recognition and self-esteem. She was taught that with the right presentation and a positive attitude, she could get whatever she wanted.

Pam had drive and intelligence, but she had only half the equation. She knew what she wanted, but she was not at all tuned in to the needs of others. Her classmates listened to her because she was a hot babe, but they didn't take her seriously—at least not as seriously as she wanted. Pam did not lack ambition, but guys couldn't get past her body. She made a presentation to the Pep Club about putting on a car wash to raise money, but the meeting disintegrated when the guys started asking her if she was going to wear a bikini. She was insulted by that, and rightfully so

Pam had a need to lead, but the totally testosteroned teenage guys couldn't get beyond her looks. It confused and frustrated her, which caused her to stress out and overeat. When guys started commenting that she was getting a "JaLo butt," Pam was filled with conflicting emotions. She had basked in the attention her looks attracted, but she had felt that nobody respected her intelligence. Then she became depressed and bulimic, bingeng and purging and throwing her health into ruin. She felt she was losing her popularity and her status, even though she was uncomfortable that those were based mostly on her physical appearance. She started obsessing about it, buying every self-help book on the market, listening to motivational tapes, and going to "personal power" seminars. She was a prom queen who'd lost her crown, and she was frantic to get it back.

Does this story remind you of anyone you know? Pam was needy with a capital N. Her needs for recognition and validation as a serious person weren't being met, so she went into crisis mode.

Look around you, and you will see this scenario in every part of society. In the self-help classes that Pam went to, you are taught that if you know what you want, you will get it as long as you work at it and don't give up. That's crap. You can't demand success. Teaching that you can is what I call a "direct act of neglect." It is neglect because the world does not work that way. You may bully or seduce someone to get your way, but there is no long-term fulfillment in that.

My dad has taught hundreds of people how to do "need-satisfaction salesmanship," which is all about developing connections with other people. I think the same principles work in all relationships. You have to know what a person wants before you can sell to his needs. The same holds true when you want to connect to your parents or teen. You have to listen to what *they* want before you can respond to *their* needs. If you are totally absorbed in your own wants and needs, you'll never connect with the other person. You'll be like Pam—all needs, no deeds. If you don't listen to the other side, they'll hang up on you like a wrong number.

Plugging In to the Other Side

How can you find out what another person's needs are? It's not easy. Just asking him or her won't do it. Most people don't do introspection at the drop of a hat. Ask them what their needs are, and you'll most likely get a superficial or smart-aleck answer like "A million dollars." Even someone who does have a handle on his needs is not likely to tell you in casual conversation. Most people have a need for privacy in that regard, and they expect you to respect it.

I have two approaches for getting to know someone's needs. Method I involves getting others to go through the same procedure you did in the previous chapter and then asking them what their answers were. Or I fill out the forms according to what you think their needs are and then ask them if you're right.

Method I

The easiest approach to discovering the needs of your parent or teen is to invite the person to fill out the "Basic Needs Assessment" below. Tell them, "I want to reconnect with you. I think the way to do that is to better understand you and your needs. I have taken this Basic Needs Assessment questionnaire, and I will share what I learned with you if you will do the same for me. I think this will help you and me to reconnect. I want to have a better relationship with you, one that can withstand any disagreements. You can keep your copy and not show it to me, but I'd like to figure out how we can get closer."

Ask your parent or teen to take the time to follow the instructions, just as you did, but do not share your own findings right away as you may bias their responses. Allow plenty of time for the other person to consider all the options or to add some, if necessary.

161

Basic Needs Assessment

This is a survey of your deeper emotional needs as opposed to your more superficial wants. The folks on Madison Avenue would like you to believe that your most basic need is a Sony PlayStation or a GE microwave, but those are just material things. They may satisfy your wants, but they won't give you the deeper satisfaction demanded by your emotional needs. Once you identify your most basic needs, you'll understand yourself better. If you know what you need, it's easier to form relationships that meet those needs. The needs that add real value to our lives can generally be classified as those related to:

- Belonging
- Security
- Self-esteem
- Vocational or artistic expression
- Love and affection

I have grouped needs into these five categories, but some of the needs fit under more than one category. If you don't see your need under one category, look for it somewhere else or write it down. I once had a woman say that she needed to trust people more. This need wasn't on the list I provided, so she wrote, "I need to write a new category because I have a need in the category of needing to trust people more, uncategorically." She also had a need to be a smart aleck.

Check off all the needs you feel now, both the ones you think are being met and the ones you feel are not being met.

Safety and Physical Needs

1. (   ) The need to know that my family is safe physically
2. (   ) The need to know that my family is safe from psychological or social harm
3. (   ) The need to be touched as a sign of support, care, and approval
4. (   ) The need to feel physically welcomed with a hug, a handshake, a kiss, or a pat on the back
5. (   ) The need to have appropriate clothing for my situation
6. (   ) The need to have transportation and ways of getting to places
7. (   ) The need to feel safe from physical abuse
8. (   ) The need to feel safe from abusive psychological behavior

9. ( ) The need to have a place for reflection
10. ( ) The need not to suffer humiliation from my family
11. ( ) Others:

Belonging Needs

1. ( ) The need to feel a sense of belonging
2. ( ) The need to know I've been forgiven
3. ( ) The need to feel accepted with all my flaws and faults
4. ( ) The need to know I have close friends
5. ( ) The need for family connections
6. ( ) The need to feel welcomed and wanted by my family
7. ( ) The need to be emotionally connected
8. ( ) The need to be part of a team
9. ( ) The need to be treated with courtesy and politeness
10. ( ) The need to share joy and fun
11. ( ) Others:

Security Needs

1. ( ) The need to feel valued by my family
2. ( ) The need to be supported in times of distress, conflict, or embarrassment
3. ( ) The need to know that someone will rally to my side when he or she is needed
4. ( ) The need to know that I can get guidance when I am out of control and confused
5. ( ) The need to know that someone will protect me when I am threatened
6. ( ) The need to feel loyalty
7. ( ) The need to feel commitment
8. ( ) The need to know that I have a place to go when my world falls apart
9. ( ) The need for a relationship that will hold up regardless of disagreements or confrontations
10. ( ) The need for security
11. ( ) Others:

163

Self-Esteem Needs

1. (   ) The need to be respected
2. (   ) The need to have be appreciated for my service to others
3. (   ) The need to feel important
4. (   ) The need to feel special
5. (   ) The need to feel that my family is proud of me
6. (   ) The need to be trusted to make good decisions
7. (   ) The need for appreciation
8. (   ) The need for nonverbal encouragement such as nods, smiles, high fives, etc.
9. (   ) The need to be proud of my accomplishments
10. (   ) The need to display and share my accomplishments
11. (   ) Others:

Vocational/Expression Needs

1. (   ) The need to explore my talents
2. (   ) The need to try new things
3. (   ) The need to express myself
4. (   ) The need to plan a career
5. (   ) The need to plan my marriage and family life
6. (   ) The need to explore lifestyle options
7. (   ) The need to focus on the demands of my vocation or special interests
8. (   ) The need to take responsibility for my life
9. (   ) The need to want something better in life
10. (   ) The need to use my talents and passions in my vocation
11. (   ) Others:

Affection needs

1. (   ) The need to feel and be told that I'm loved
2. (   ) The need to feel needed
3. (   ) The need to feel that I am a priority in someone's life
4. (   ) The need to feel that I am special to someone
5. (   ) The need to feel that someone else takes pride in my accomplishments

6. (   ) The need to be heard
7. (   ) The need to be understood
8. (   ) The need to share joy and happiness with someone
9. (   ) The need to share sadness and depression with someone
10. (   ) The need to be wanted by someone
11. (   ) Others:

Evaluation of Basic Needs Assessment

You now have lists of your needs. On those lists, a rating of 0% to 100% to indicate how well your parents or teen is meeting those needs. For example, if you need to feel loved and your family is totally meeting this need, put down 100%. Since we are discussing your parents or teen, you may want to be specific to that person in terms of how well they are meeting your needs. If you feel that a need is being met only halfway, put down 50%, and if you feel that none of that need is being addressed, put down 0%.

Need	Percentage Met by Family
1.	
2.	
3.	
4.	
5.	
6.	
7.	
8.	
9.	
10.	

165

This method requires you to make some judgments about your parent or teen's needs before proceeding. If you are lucky enough to have your partner fill out the needs questionnaire at the same time and you both went through Chapter 11, you can proceed to the next chapter. However, if you are the only participant, turn to the Basic Needs Assessment and check off the needs you think might be relevant. Again, do not try to eliminate any need just because I categorized it under another label.

Don't rush through this process of checking off others' needs. Do a little detective work and observe what the others say or do. Maybe you can ask them about their needs: "You said yesterday that you needed that money. Why did you say you needed it? Do you have some plans for it? Are you feeling depressed? Do you want to buy something and make yourself feel better, or are you feeling a little unsatisfied now?"

If they look as though they're going to smack you for playing "psychologist," duck and resume your plan later. Try to discover their priorities in their behaviors. If they have only a few dollars, what do they spend it on? What are their goals? What kinds of movies or books do they like? What kinds of friends do they have?

These are ideas for learning other people's needs. If you are the teen looking for your parents' needs, let me give you a starter list. The number one need for parents is safety. They want to know that their kids are safe—a windowless padded room surrounded by armed guards is the setting of choice. Their number two parent need is acceptance. I know it sounds weird, but parents want their teens to accept them. They want the connection. Their third greatest need is respect. Your parents feel they've worked to make your life comfortable. They feel they deserve credit and respect for that.

Okay, I've given you some starting points. Now you're on your own. If your needs are not listed, make them up. For you parents trying to guess what your teen's needs are, here are some hints. Our first need is acceptance. We want to know that you accept us unconditionally, no matter what body parts we've pierced or tattooed, no matter how low our jeans ride on our hips or how high our T-shirt rides above our belly button. We know we seem strange to you; sometimes we seem strange to ourselves. But we need your loyalty, which is number two on our need hit parade. Number three is support. We want you to be proud of us, but to be proud of us as we are right now—even if you think we are whacked out. We want you to support us in all of our craziness. It's part of our quest to find out who we are. You'll be glad to know that we don't expect you to stand by and watch us do something that could endanger our lives or hurt our reputation for years to come. Even if we really, really want to do it.

I've given you a push, so keep rolling and finish this list of needs on your own.

The next step does require some dialogue with the other person. You've done the best you can, but you can do only so much. It's time for a summit meeting. Tell your parents or teens that you have an offer they can't refuse. You want to reconnect with them and build a stronger relationship than you've ever had. But you need their full attention to get things rolling.

Tell them that you've made both mistakes and misjudgments, mostly because you haven't understood each other very well. You want to change the way you deal with each other. But to do that, you want to build a relationship that meets the needs of both sides.

Mention that you've put together a checklist with your thoughts on what your parents' or teens' needs are. You can either give them the list or read their needs aloud for their responses as to the accuracy of your guesses. Ask if there are any other needs they'd suggest. List the needs approved and suggested by your parents or teens.

Don't rush; let them take as long as they need. Hopefully, you will learn a lot from this. Listen well. Finally, have your parents or teens rate how each need is being met on the 0% to 100% scale. Talk with your parents or teens about how you can better meet those needs that are not being met satisfactorily now.

167

We're into the heavy stuff now. Later you will put this information to good use, but even at this stage you are beginning to reconnect just by communicating your needs to each other.

The Needs of Others—Ground Rules

If you are ever going to have a satisfying relationship, you have to respect and maintain the "sacred space" in which you share intimate secrets and thoughts. It is a serious responsibility to share someone's secrets. When your parent or teen gives you that sort of trust, you must treat it carefully. This holds true especially for teens, because we tend to become uncomfortable when our parents share their feelings with us, and we turn goofy.

Your parent or teen is vulnerable now, so you should never, ever consider using this intimate information as a weapon against him or her in an argument or disagreement. This may be very difficult because it is easy to hurt another person by using the information he or she has provided you. But it's also the lowest of blows. Intimate information is not leverage. It is not a weapon to use against another person. It is nothing to joke or tease about. It is a tremendous responsibility. You risk damaging your relationship if you betray the confidence of your parent or teen at this delicate stage of the reconnection process.

This is no time to be judgmental. This is extremely important for parents. Teens live in a hothouse environment. Their emotions and feelings run amok. Everything is intensified for them. And what may seem a small matter to you can be a major crisis from the teen perspective. On the other hand, the threat of losing a job, for example, does not seem to be nearly as important to a teen as it does to the parent. The overall principle here is to treat each person's intimate world as kindly as possible. Don't judge; instead, try to understand. If the other person knows you understand his or her needs, he or she will open up to you and welcome a relationship.

Wendy was in a class ahead of me. Everyone liked her, and they liked her mother even more. Wendy's mother was one of the kindest people in town. She was beloved because she was an Olympic-level listener. Teens would go over to Wendy's house and talk to her mom for hours. Her popularity proved that teens want to talk to adults, it's just that they don't feel most adults will listen to them. Wendy's mom did.

I was one of the teens who talked to her for hours. I talked to her about my car, my girlfriend, my basketball ambitions. She really seemed to care. She was unbelievably gracious with her time. She listened, and she kept quiet about what she heard. I bet she could write ten novels based on the things teens told her. Two girls in my high school got pregnant. They told Wendy's mom before they told their own. She was also the only adult in town to know who had shot the old mule in the principal's office—a world-class prank from my high school days. I don't think the Sopranos could have forced that information out of Wendy's mom. She observed the code of silence.

Wendy's mom should be a model for all parents. She closed the gap of years and experience simply by listening without judging, by giving of her time, by showing genuine concern and interest. Most of all, she gave teens her respect and friendship. She understood our needs completely, and she respected them.

Relationships are built on trust and respect. Take this step slowly, and enjoy the sense that connections are being made. Give your relationship time now, and watch as the gap that once seemed so vast slowly begins to close. Wounds heal when given proper care. The doctor is in the house.

169

13

JUST SAY "WHY NOT?"

A Letter to Parents

Dear Parents,

In this chapter, I am going to give your teen some specific instructions, and I want you to understand that he or she is going to be asking you something based on my suggestion. I'm instructing your teen to ask you a question whenever you say "No." I want your teen to ask for the reasoning behind your decision so that he or she can understand the process of making good decisions. So when your teen says "Why not?" it is not meant as a challenge to your authority, nor is it the typical teen tactic of trying to wear you down to get the answer he wants. Please work with me on this. The goal of this method is to give your teen a basis for making her own good decisions in the future by opening up the lines of communication between the more mature and experienced parent and the teen.

One of the primary goals of this book is to help your teen understand your needs better. From now on, when he or she asks "Why not?" the goal is to find out which of your needs is behind the decision. Of course the primary parental need, your child's safety, will be the usual reason. Your child needs to hear that because it teaches her the responsibilities of parenting and it also gives your teen further evidence that she is loved and valued.

Suppose your teen comes to you and asks if he or she can go to a movie that lets out at 1 A.M., and you oppose this idea with a "No." "Why not?" is the prescribed response. If you are worried about the safety of your teen at that hour, you might say, "I think that it is unsafe." If you think that he or she broke some contract with you by not taking out the trash or failing to make a certain grade, you might say, "You cannot go because you did not uphold your end of the contract when you did not take out the trash [did not make the grades we agreed on]."

Your teen's next move will be to try to meet your needs. Again, this is part of my instructions. Listen to her. You do not have to change your mind, but talk to her about what you want. This may become a negotiation, and this is good for both of you. If you can't come to terms, that's okay; at least you both talked about your needs.

Feel free to turn the tables on your teen and ask him "Why not?" too. He may surprise you and open up about his needs, giving you the opportunity to learn more about what goes on inside his mind in this exciting but often confusing and emotionally charged time in his life.

Good luck reconnecting with each other.

Thanks,

Jay

In this chapter I am going to give you some great information on how to negotiate with your parent or teen in order to reach a "settlement" that meets the needs of both of you. You'll be glad to know that this is designed to be a pain-free process. No screaming. No door slamming. No blood. No foul.

Negotiation is the key to reconnecting with your parent or teen. So many of the worst conflicts in your relationship arise when one of you wants what the other can't, won't, or doesn't know how to give. Such situations are inevitable, even if one of you is Teen Angel and the other is Perfect Parent. By giving you the tools to negotiate with your parent or teen, I am helping you find a way to resolve those situations without hurting or being hurt. The goal is to create a win-win resolution so that both sides are satisfied that they've been heard and treated fairly.

Negotiating in a relationship isn't about manipulating the other person. It's about being in control of the process rather than letting your emotions control you. It's not about taking something from the person on the other side of the table. You don't sit down to a family meal and "take" food from each other. You share. Each person takes what he wants while also making sure that the others get fed too. That's what you are going to learn to do in your parent-teen negotiations.

As I have this famous psychologist and relationship expert in my family, I've had a lot of friends come to me for help with their parents. Joe-Tom and I were at the lake one day when he started talking about his problems with his parents: "My mom and dad really don't know what I'm doing most of the time. I think they're just counting down the days until I'm gone, waiting for me to get out of their hair. That's the way I've started to feel. I'm just marking time. We don't have anything in common. They've never smoked dope or snorted cocaine. They were probably virgins when they married. My dad even told me that he didn't have a car until he graduated from college. What can they teach me? I'm pretty much on my own already."

Joe-Tom and his parents are staring at each other across the Grand Canyon. Neither one knows how to bridge the gap, so they tell themselves it can't be done. But the fact that Joe-Tom is talking about that lack of communication indicates that it troubles him. He wants to reconnect with his parents, but he doesn't know how to do it. Their lives and their beliefs are so different, he thinks there is no basis for communication. His wild ways could be interpreted as an effort to bridge the gap by getting into so much trouble that his parents will have to reach out to him.

Motivation and Negotiation

The art of parent-teen negotiation that I'm going to explain to you is based on sound logic and psychological principles taught to me by my father—in the family room, the kitchen, and all of the seminars and speeches I've heard him give. I've lived through the process of reconnecting through negotiation. I've never had a major parent-teen gap to contend with because my dad wouldn't let that happen. But we're a normal family, and there have been times when we've let our relationship slide. We've always found ways to reconnect.

This process isn't about manipulation as much as motivation. It's about motivating each other so that you both want the other person to walk away from the negotiation feeling satisfied and well treated. You motivate each other by providing your parent or teen with positive reinforcements every step of the way.

Money is the most common form of positive reinforcement. We work like maniacs to get some of that government-issued paper because it has value in our world. You can buy things with it to satisfy your wants and needs, so when you get it for working, it serves as a positive reinforcement. There are other reinforcers with the power to motivate human behavior. Power, pride, sex, and—from a personal standpoint—Oreo Blizzards are among the most awesome reinforces. People can be motivated to do almost anything if you put those carrots on the stick.

Spend a few hours with any family, and you can figure out what their primary reinforcers are. I did this when I was dating a lot in high school. I always tried to figure out what was important to the parents so I could get on their good side and they'd trust me to take their daughters out. If the "Joneses" talked about how much they enjoyed family vacations and watching each other participate in sports, it was safe to say that they placed a lot of value on their family relationships. If the "Smiths" showed more interest in talking about their new boat, their vacation home, or their stock portfolio, they were more focused on possessions and status as their reinforcers.

Another family that I'll call the "Allisons" regarded religion as a major reinforcer. The teens in their family were active in church youth groups, and the parents supported the church financially. It was interesting to see how families built their lives around different reinforcers. I didn't try to put one over on any of them by pretending to be what I wasn't. But I did base my "negotiations" with their daughters on whatever positive reinforcers were valued by each particular family. I asked the Jones girl to join us on family trips. I took the Smith girl to "society" parties. And I sure as holy heck didn't ask the Allisons' daughter to go out on a Sunday morning, when she was expected to be in church.

Rewards and Punishments

Some people confuse rewards and punishments with positive and negative negotiations. Rewards and punishments are ways of reinforcing behavior. Rewards are the positive reinforcers of needs. Punishments are the negative reinforcers. You get people to do what you want by either rewarding them or punishing them. If your teenage student goofs off, you charge up the cattle prod and apply it to the body part of choice. (Caution: This is intended to be taken as humorous exaggeration. Jay McGraw & Company do not advocate the use of torture in parent-teen relationships.)

175

How do teens punish their parents? By withholding their love and approval. Believe it. You parents don't want to be on your bad side. They want to have a good relationship with you. And now we're going to look at how to make that happen without inflicting pain on either party.

The Art of Parent-Teen Negotiations

The key feature of negotiation is to find out what you can do to make the other person happier and to do it in such a way that the other person will want to make you happier too. I'm talking a whole lot of happy here, and I'm happy as hell to do it. The route to happiness in negotiation is directly through the eardrum, past your hammer, anvil, and stirrup, and on to your brain. I'm talking ears here. Nothing like a whopping good set of ears for reconnecting with your parent or teen. Open ears. Ears with a direct link to the brain's center of comprehension and understanding.

Just as I listened carefully to my dates' parents to find out what their reinforcers were, you should do the same with your parent or teen. For example, does your dad get more enthusiastic about your good grades or about his '65 Chevy SS? Does your mother seem more pleasant when you tell her that you sang her favorite song in choir or when you compliment her on her taste in clothes? Does your father relax more with you when you go fishing with him? Does your teen respond better when you suggest that if he cleans the garage you'll take him to look at some new wheels for his car?

Your parent or teen is constantly putting out signals that communicate his or her needs and priorities. All you have to do is train yourself to listen. You broadcast your own "switches and knobs" too. The things that turn you on or off become obvious in your conversations and in the way you live. If you like to be the center of attention, that becomes obvious in the volume of your voice, the way you walk into a room, and where you position yourself in a group of people.

Once you understand the other person's reinforcers and needs, anything can be negotiated. Know it and believe it. There is a way, but you have to put some effort into it. If you take the lazy route, it leads to fatalistic thinking: "It doesn't matter what I do or say because they're not ever going to change, ever do any different, ever see any different.

They're hardheaded, and they'll never go for it." That's chicken bleep. It's loser talk.

That sort of crap is put out by people who simply do not understand how to negotiate for what they want. You don't sit down and negotiate a deal by saying "Okay, Frank, here's the deal. You do all the work, and I'll take all the money and credit." Even if you were able to cut that fat hog of a deal for some reason (you have hypnotic powers? the other person is brain dead?) how long do you think the agreement would hold up?

One-sided agreements have a tendency to dissolve into thin air. The person stuck on the wrong side of the agreement will do a meltdown sooner or later, probably sooner. His or her needs are not being met. Translation: He's getting screwed—and that's a surefire guarantee that the agreement won't stick.

To negotiate a win-win situation, you have to come up with an agreement you can both be excited about. If one side simply caves in during negotiations because the other side has beaten him or her into submission, you haven't negotiated, you've administered a butt kicking. And nobody wakes up after a butt kicking and says, "Damn, that *still* feels good!" A well-negotiated agreement leaves both parties feeling that, all in all, they came out with some of what they wanted without having to give up a lot.

> **Teen:** Mom, I want a later curfew. I want to come home at one A.M. instead of twelve. All my friends are all still out having fun when I have to go home. They make fun of me for having a little kid's curfew.

> **Mom:** Hey, I read in *The National Enquirer* that seventy percent of car accidents happen between midnight and one A.M. I don't want my teen on the streets at that hour with all the whacked-out drivers looking for a crash-test dummy.

The mother is saying that her son's "need" to be out until 1 A.M. is in conflict with her "need" to know that he is safe.

Is this conflict negotiable? Sure, if both sides approach it with an understanding of the other's needs.

Mom: "I am willing to extend your curfew under one of two conditions. One, you can bring your friends here at midnight and they can stay all night. Or you can stay all night with a friend whose parents I know. You call me at midnight and let me know you are safe and that there are parents home. It's not that I want to control you, it's that I need to know you are safe.

The teen may not be entirely happy with this proposal. Maybe he wants to hang out with his friends at a dance or pizza joint until 1 A.M. If that's the case, the mother could offer to pick him up at that hour so she knows he will have a safe ride home. There are dozens of ways to resolve this conflict of needs, but only if both sides are willing to communicate and negotiate.

Each parent-teen negotiation should be approached in the following step-by-step manner.

1. Figure out what it is you really want. Keep it simple. No multiple demands. One, maybe two things at the most. Communicate the feelings behind your needs: "I want to stay out until one A.M. so I can feel part of the group. I don't want to feel like an outsider."

Don't be rigid in your demands or your thinking. There are a lot of ways to get what you want. (Hint: Don't use ultimatums in making your needs known. People tend to throw their hands up in the air and order a massive bomb drop when confronted with ultimatums.)

2. Put as much effort into defining the other side's needs as you put into defining and communicating your own. You should be able to express what the other person wants as clearly as he or she expresses it: "Now, let me see if I've got this right. You want me to come home at midnight because you're worried that something bad could happen to me on the way home at a later hour, right?"

3. Structure the agreement so that you can both feel excited about it and you both understand your obligations. Don't try to control other people's thinking. You want them to walk away feeling as though they

had a hand on the wheel too. When you share control of the process, the other side takes co-ownership of the deal and there is less likelihood that one of you will feel used or abused.

Parents: It's in your best interest to build a sense of self-determination and control in your teens. As long as you allow them to feel that they've had some control in the decision-making process, they're likely to accept the final agreement even if they don't get exactly what they wanted.

One of the ways you can get people to do things they really don't want to do is to sweeten the pot. "If you want to go out with your friends, you have to do the dishes." Why would they do the dishes? So they can go out with their friends. You've tied their desire to do something desirable—go out with friends—to doing something less desirable—doing the dishes. There may be some moaning and whining involved, but normally they'll do the dumb dishes so they can go have some fun. It's easier for them to swallow because it puts them in control: If I do the dishes, I get to go out.

That's a little behavioral psychology thrown in at no extra charge. The key to using this method is to be careful when you are negotiating the price the teen has to pay to get what he wants. It's terribly unfair to expect a natural C student to make Bs in order to get something she wants. You have to be realistic and fair. You wouldn't say, "You're getting grounded if it rains" because your teen doesn't control the weather. Don't set the bar so high that it fouls the deal or dooms the teen to failure. You want to program your teens for success so they can support you in your golden years.

It's important to set out the terms of the agreement clearly so there is no wiggle room if either party fails to live up to them. If you've negotiated an agreement that allows your teen to go to a party Friday night as long as he gets all of his homework done on time, make sure that he understands the consequences if he fails to live up to his obligations. That way, there shouldn't be much ground for whining if he doesn't get the work done.

Parent: I'm sorry you did that to yourself, but you know the consequences, I
           didn't fail to turn in your homework, you did. I'm just the gate-
           keeper, and you don't have a ticket.

It's Okay to Say, "Why Not?"

Teens: I'm going to give you a phrase that will open up your communications with your parent. At the beginning of this chapter, I gave them
a letter that will clue them in what to expect from you so they don't hyperventilate or blow an aortic valve. If they haven't read it yet, have
them read it. What I propose is that you begin asking the question
"Why not?" every time you get a "No" when you ask for something.
You may get slammed the first couple of times. If that happens, talk to
your parents and assure them you aren't being a smart-ass and you
aren't trying to wear them down. You are trying to learn how they
make their decisions so you can learn to make them on your own one
day. Tell them you want to understand their needs so you can respond
to them better.

The bottom line is that you want to open up communications. Once
you establish that your intention is to reconnect with them—and once
you've proven that your intention is honorable—you should be able to
build mutual trust and cooperation.

Once you've had some practice in the real world of parent-teen
negotiations, the methods I've outlined in this chapter should help
you build a much better relationship, one that will grow stronger with
time.

Most problems in relationships are caused by a lack of communication and understanding. When you listen with the goal of
truly understanding each other's needs and then work to fulfill
them, it eliminates many of the conflicts that plague parents and
teens.

This book is about connection and relationship. If you want a better relationship with your teen or parent, these steps will take you there. The next step is yours. The ideas and methods I've laid out so far will take you only up to the door. It's up to you to grab the handle and turn it.

14

TEN WAYS TO BRIDGE THE GAP AND RECONNECT

In my high school basketball days, it bothered me that I was always at my best at the end of the season. Every year I could see from my stats that my game picked up considerably in the final weeks. Eventually I figured it out: I wasn't playing much ball or practicing during the off-season. As a result, my skills went down the tubes.

I've learned that you can't slack off when it comes to maintaining your relationships either. If you don't work on your skills all the time, you lose your game. As my dad might say, "Relationships ain't ham. They are managed, not cured."

So how can you manage a relationship once you've figured out all of the dos and don'ts, myths, poisons, land mines, and all the other stuff I've been laying on you for the last thirteen chapters? How can you get the ball rolling?

I know that getting started will be hard; it always is. But remember that old cliché about the snowball effect: getting the core to stick together may be hard, but once you get it rolling, big things happen.

To help you roll into your reconnected relationship with your parents or teens, I've come up with ten ways to bridge the gap. You can play the games I've suggested with each other as a family or just with two of you. These games are supposed to bring you together in a relaxed and enjoyable way. They're icebreakers. You still cannot afford

183

to coast in your relationship. You've got to get involved and hang on. It's a lot of work, but if you put in the time and effort—and love—one day your parent-teen relationship will develop into the sort of parent-adult relationship that will bring you happiness and fulfillment for the rest of your lives.

1. Let's Catch a Flick, Nick

Invite your parents or teen to a night at the movies and then do the thumbs-up and thumbs-down thing together. Do it for at least two weeks, watching a movie a week. Each of you gets a turn to pick the flick. Have some popcorn too. Easy on the butter.

Don't just watch the movies and then go your separate ways. Have a pizza or a couple of sodas afterward and discuss what the movie meant to you and how you related to the characters. Learn a little bit about each other in the process. You don't have to agree. Give it a thumbs-up or thumbs-down, but talk about why you feel what you feel. Talk about what values the movie presented and about whether the plot had any particular relevance to your life.

Let Me Tell You a Story

A friend of mine did this with his parents for almost five years. Every Thursday night they would watch a movie together. Each person would have the responsibility of finding a movie important to him or her. The parent would often pick a classic movie like *Rebel Without a Cause* or *Mutiny on the Bounty*. The teen would choose something like *Raiders of the Lost Ark* or *American Beauty*. Regardless of what they chose, there was a lot of discussion.

The Bottom Line

Your movie date will bring you together as a family for at least three hours a week and give you both the opportunity to set the schedule for at least a portion of each other's day—and who knows, you may even learn a little about each other.

2. Tell 'Em What You Like, Mike

In this game, each of you writes down three things that you really like about the other person. Then you exchange your pieces of paper. Just read them and let the words sink in for a few days without talking about what was written. The idea isn't to give instant pats on the back, it's to build each other's confidence and trust.

Let Me Tell You a Story

This is one of the most remarkable exercises to do. You see, it is my hypothesis that we never tell each other what we like about each other because we are so busy telling each other what we don't like. Sometimes people have to really think of what to say. I remember one family that was totally changed when they did this exercise. The teen kept telling me about it over and over: "I can't believe that my dad likes my jokes. I know most of them are pretty dumb, but he said he likes them! How cool is that?" He told me that he had started telling more jokes and the family kept laughing at them. I hear he has tried out his act at some comedy clubs. Who can tell where this will go?

The Bottom Line

We may think that someone likes nothing about us, when in reality they just don't feel comfortable complimenting us. A parent might be afraid the teen will let it go to his head. Playing this game will clear that up so that when you feel as if your teen or your parents hate you, you can always pull these out as proof that they don't. This game will really get the ball rolling toward a better experience at home.

3. Deal, Neal

Playing cards is a very social way to spend some time together—unless one of you catches the other cheating, of course. If you teach each other a card game and play at least two sets, you'll share the teacher-student role and learn a little about each other in the process. Cards are a great equalizer because luck plays such a role in what hand you are dealt. Each of you can learn something new from the other, and you can display your cardsharp skills at the game you play the best.

Let Me Tell You a Story

Can you believe that Dania's father had never heard of Dirty Eight? Dania had never seen him laugh so hard in her life, regardless of whether he won or not. It was a relief that he could do something with his daughter besides making rules and having to back them up with some kind of wisdom he didn't have. Now they have a regular poker game because it's the one way Dania can get money from her dad without having to work for it.

The Bottom Line

Creative interactions are what keep your relationships from getting stuck in the mud. There will always be arguments and differences of opinion, and there will always be new problems. That's why you can keep a relationship fresh with a good game of cards.

4. Take a Hike, Mike

Take an imaginary trip with each other. Decide that you are going on a trek that will present you with some major obstacles, such as crossing a river and dealing with wild boars. Talk about how each of you would handle the challenges. For example, consider the following pilgrimage: You are going to hike a section of the Appalachian Trail, and you will be gone for three weeks. You will be carrying your own materials, so take some time and decide what you would take. (Take five minutes to contemplate your responses.)

Before answering, consider that you are required to get from one side of a river to the other. How would you accomplish this feat? (Take five minutes to consider.)

Now consider that you have to get past a giant ogre in your path. How would you do it? (Take five minutes.)

Now consider that you have returned home and you want to celebrate. How would you want to celebrate? Have your friends over? Celebrate by yourself? Celebrate with a special friend? (Take five minutes.)

Now discuss each decision and compare how each of you would handle these problems. Recognize each other's creativity and unique approaches.

Let Me Tell You a Story

I know a family who did this journey-of-the-mind thing, and when they went through their choices, they were amazed at each other's creativity and insights. They were especially interested in each other's preferences for celebration. The teen did not know that his parents treasured celebrating things together. In fact, he had forgotten that they had ever celebrated anything together.

The Bottom Line

Imagery is a valuable way of stimulating the mind and conversation between people who have forgotten how to talk to each other. With this exercise, parents and teens come to appreciate each other's creativity and imagination.

5. Tackle a Taboo, Mary Lou

187

It's a shame that people don't want to discuss important issues anymore. Topics such as politics and religion are all but taboo in "polite" society. How can young people ever learn about their parents' values? How can they learn to respect that everyone has the right to an opinion, whether it is popular or not? Take some time and compare your answers to these scenarios and questions:

1. You're a brilliant scientist, and you hold the formula that will cure cancer. The only problem is that you will have to sacrifice one of your children to save the rest. What would you do?

2. You're the captain of a ship, and the boat is sinking. You can save all the passengers if someone jumps overboard. A woman and man both volunteer. What is your choice?

3. You're single, and you've fallen in love with someone who tells you that he/she will marry you but doctors have diagnosed him/her with cancer. Your loved one has only six months to live. What would you do? What if the person was not dying but still planned to leave you in six months. Would your view of this change?

Let Me Tell You a Story

These values-clarification stories really inspire a lot of discussion and emotions. A teen friend told me that she felt really good about expressing her feelings in this type of session. It wasn't so much that she felt strongly about the issues. It was more that she felt a passion for talking about her feelings on topics with more depth than who was on the cover of last week's *People* magazine.

The Bottom Line

Often we don't know how we feel about an issue until we talk about it. This is a good exercise for discovering something about yourself as well as the people you care about. And talking to each other is good, very good, because if you can talk about the little things, the lines will be open when something really important comes up.

6. Play for a Win-Win, Lynn and Sven

We play all kinds of games as children, but as adults we tend to place far too much emphasis on winning. That takes a lot of the joy out of play. I suggest you play games in which you both win. Do you remember paper, rock, scissors? It's the game where one player tries to guess what the other is going to signal with his hand. I've redesigned that game so nobody loses. Instead of paper, rock, or scissors on count three, you display a number of fingers from two to five. If the sum of your combined show of fingers is seven, you both win and you give each other something, like a dime, a piece of candy, or just a pat on the back.

Let Me Tell You a Story

A father and his teenage son played a game of tennis in which the only objective was to keep the ball in play. The Guinness world record is 6,001 rallies in a regular tennis match. They had 5,000 the last time I heard. When you see them play, it is an inspiration. Instead of competing, they holler encouragement at each other and cheer each other on. You gotta like a game like that!

The Bottom Line

Be on the same side and make your game a win-win.

7. Check Out My 'Zine, Colleen

Switch your favorite magazines with your parent or teen to share things from your own worlds. You might be surprised by the curiosity these articles inspire, especially the advertisements. It also helps each of you understand the issues that are important to the other.

Let Me Tell You a Story

I have two stories. One father really enjoyed his daughter's magazine because it had a lot of stories on how to deal with tough fathers. He wanted to read her magazines to know how to defend himself. He also confessed that his daughter must have been pretty smart to read such a sophisticated magazine.

My second story is of a daughter who got engrossed in her father's bowling magazine. She got into it so much that she joined a father-daughter bowling league. They became bowling buddies, and their relationship was on a roll.

The Bottom Line

This is another great way to open the lines of dialogue and communication. Sharing interests increases understanding.

189

8. Play an Old Part, Bart

Watch some corny old movies together, but turn off the sound and choose a character. Each of you fills in the lines according to what you think is going on. You might choose opposite characters, with the teen playing an older person and the parent doing a younger one. The whole family can get into this one. It's a laugh fest to hear what people come up with.

Let Me Tell You a Story

I cannot tell you how often or how hard this game has made me laugh. My ribs ached the last time I played it. It has also given me some good insights into what makes my mom and dad tick. Sometimes it's a little scary how the old movie plots echo what is really going on in the news—or in the family room. Dad and I were feuding once when we starting playing this game with an old western on television. It came to the big climax where the two gunslingers were getting ready for a gun duel. One stared at the other, and I supplied the line "So it's come to this, has it?" My dad then spoke up for the other gunslinger, saying "You just can't take a joke, can you?"

I broke up, and he did too. We laughed at their standoff, and in the process we broke our own.

The Bottom Line

Have a little fun playing different roles, using old movies as setups in conflicts or other dynamics to discover each other's creativity and shifts in perceptions.

9. Do Some Supportin', Norton

If one of the parents or the teen is trying to kick a habit or practice a little self-discipline, the other side offers either to join in the plan or to do something similar. For example, if your teen needs to go on a diet, you could do the diet too, or you could give up smoking at the same time. Or if your parent wants to get in better shape, you could join in the workout every day. This is a very powerful win-win sort of bonding. You know the old saying: Families that strive together, thrive together.

Let Me Tell You a Story

My friend Sally had developed a pretty significant alcohol problem. I couldn't be around her anymore because she was so out of control with it. Her mother stepped in and made a contract with her. Since the mother was overweight and a diabetic, she said she would give up all sweets if Sally would give up booze. It was hard on them both, but they made it because they did it for each other.

The Bottom Line

It's one thing to say, "I support you." It's another thing to join in the battle and make sacrifices alongside your family member. Life is a team sport, and this is a great way to reconnect with your parent or teen.

10. Wanna Win a Prize, Guys?

How about entering a contest together? Everybody's a winner in this game. I wanted to do this exercise with my folks, but I couldn't find many contests for parents and teens. So I made some up. You can find them on my Web site at www.jaymcgraw.com. Come play for the big bucks and reconnect with your family.

The Bottom Line

I believe so much in this, I've put up prizes for it. There are more pay-offs here than you might imagine. See you on the Web at www.jaymc graw.com.

191

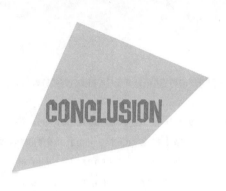

CONCLUSION

Letter to Parents

Dear Parents,

First, if you have actually read this entire book, as opposed to skipping ahead to this letter, *and* you have done all of the work in the book, I would like to say, Great work and congratulations! You have just taken a *huge* step toward improving your life at home. However, while you have worked hard and made enormous improvements, your job is not over just yet. There will be problems in your relationship with your teens from this point on, just as there have been in the past. The difference now is that you are better prepared to deal with the problems that will arise. Bottom line: Don't freak out when you have your first "post-book" fight. I can promise you this: It *will* happen.

Second, I would like to beg and plead on behalf of every teen in America that you please please *please* be flexible with your teens. We will make some pretty dumb mistakes—let's just call them youthful indiscretions (that sounds better)—but that doesn't mean we are completely brain dead. The next time your teen buries himself or herself in a hole, give him or her a chance to climb back out. We are terrified to make mistakes because we're afraid we'll never live them down. We are not code-named "Damien." We are not spawns of the devil. If your teen lies, cheats, steals, breaks curfew, or blows off schoolwork, then, by all means mete out some punishment. Just don't make it a life sentence. If we feel as if we can't climb out of the hole we're in, we may quit trying.

Bottom line: Long-term punishments are not effective; predictable punishments are.

Third, reward your teen for good behavior, and that includes reading this book. If your teen has taken the time and energy to try to improve your relationship, reward him or her for it. He or she deserves it. Bottom line: If you reward us for good behavior, you will see a lot more of it in the future.

Finally, have some fun together! I can tell you that although we may not always show it, we *do* enjoy spending time with you. We don't always want to be on your bad side; we want to share more good times while getting to know each other better. Bottom line: Lighten up and enjoy some time together.

Thanks for reading, and best of luck,
Jay

P.S. Please e-mail me with any of your questions through my website at www.JayMcGraw.com

Letter to Teens

Dear Teens,

Jay asked me to write a letter to you "young-'uns" while he wrote one to your parents, so here it goes.

As a parent, I have often said: "Moms and dads are only as happy as their saddest child." That means we have a huge stake in how your life is going.

For the most part, we do care very deeply about you kids, and yes, you are kids, at least in our eyes. The truth is, as parents we are scared to death. We are scared that we have made such humongous mistakes that we have crippled you. We are scared that we have not made you feel special enough about yourself. We are afraid that you can't or won't say "No way, back off" when someone is offering you something that will put you in harm's way like drugs, alcohol, irresponsible sex, or other behaviors that are dangerous.

Look, we aren't your friends, we aren't here to tell you what you want to hear. We are here to see around corners and keep you safe until you can do it yourself. If you would join us in being responsible about your safety instead of resisting us, we would both get a whole lot more of what we want.

Friends come and go. No matter what promises you make to each other, the chance that your friends, boyfriends, or girlfriends will still be in your life in five to ten years is almost zero. The chance that your parents still will be in your life in five to ten years is almost 100 percent. Don't turn your back on the people who will be there over the long haul.

Help us know that you are safe by being a responsible partner and things will go way, way better. It's your choice, but like it or not, you and your parents are in this deal together and you might as well try to negotiate a quality, healthy, open relationship. Do your part and I predict you will like the result.

Dr. Phil McGraw

ABOUT THE AUTHOR

JAY MCGRAW is the author of the *New York Times* bestseller *Life Strategies for Teens*. He is currently enrolled at Southern Methodist University in Dallas, Texas. He enjoys spending time with his friends and his younger brother, Jordan.

Contact Jay at www.jaymcgraw.com.

Don't miss these other books by the *New York Times* bestselling author

Jay McGraw

0-7432-1546-X • $14.00

The first guide to teenage life that won't tell you what to do or who to be, but rather how to live life best.

0-7432-2470-1 • $13.00

The companion workbook to *Life Strategies for Teens*—full of quizzes, tests, and questions to help you figure out who you are and where you are going.

Available in January 2002:
Daily Life Strategies for Teens
0-7432-2471-X • $11.00

www.simonsays.com